MW01009578

Books by James Nelson

The Trouble With Gumballs
(Available in Kindle)

The Poorperson's Guide
to Great Cheap Wines

Great Wines Under $5

Killing Dave Henderson, etc.

On the Volcano

The Trouble with Gumballs

by James Nelson

THE STORY OF
AN EXPENSIVE VENTURE
INTO FREE ENTERPRISE

Published by:

Rolly Bolly Press

649 Idylberry Road

San Rafael, CA 94903

ISBN: 0-6158-4806-0
ISBN-13: 9780615848068

For the Chairman of the Board

1

"Sweetie-pie," I said to Mary-Armour one night not too long ago, "how do you suppose we got here, anyway?"

It was one of those winter evenings we have in Northern California, cold and rainy and miserable in the fields outside, but warm and toasty beside the blazing fireplace of our rented farmhouse. I was lolling, shoeless, in our easiest easy chair, staring morosely into the flames. Mary-Armour was sitting on the sofa working away at the tan sweater she'd been knitting for me ever since our courtship days.

At my question she looked up and smiled, which was quite a heart-warming sight.

"How did we get here?" she echoed. "You mean, did the stork bring us?"

"Listen," I said. "I mean, how come did we leave New York and everything?"

"Oh, that," Mary-Armour said gently. "I'm not exactly sure I remember."

"Neither do I," I said. I stood up and poked the fire with a charred stick. In return, the fire spat a glowing coal at my feet. A puff of smoke rose into the air as I kicked the coal back into the fireplace, sniffing at the familiar odor of burned rug. The fire crackled smugly.

"Sweetie," I said, "are you sorry we came?"

Mary-Armour looked up quickly and stopped knitting. "Good Lord, no!" she said. "Are you?"

"No, no," I said hastily. "No, I was just wondering how you felt about it."

"You know how I feel about it," Mary-Armour said. "Of course I'm glad we came. We have a wonderful life out here."

Then she smiled and went back to her knitting. It was really pleasant to see her sitting there, looking so doggone domestic. Who cared if she couldn't knit worth a damn?

It cheered me quite a bit, too, to hear her speak so emphatically about our new life in California. Financially, of course, our way of life was built on sand, but even so, we had *time,* which was something nobody else seemed to have, and we had two nice children, and plenty of fresh air and sunshine, and we had friends. And then, up until a few months before, we'd had this hydraheaded little business venture.

I leaned back in my chair and thought about free enterprise for a while and listened to the faint clicking of the knitting needles, and smelled the rug; and then Cleopatra, our dog, came over and needed to be petted, so I petted her awhile and thought some more about the Multivend Company, which was what our business had been called. It was a good time for thinking—peaceful, you know, with the kids already asleep, and the tempo of the rain picking up outside, and the old fire blazing away like sixty.

2

"You know," I said finally, "life is really just a great big chain reaction, isn't it?"

I saw Mary-Armour's eyebrows rise, but she kept on knitting.

"I can think of no reply to a statement like that," she said, "that wouldn't sound equally inane."

"What I mean is this," I said. "You make one little move, and you trigger a sort of Life Force that causes lots of other people to make some kind of move, and their moves trigger other Life Forces, and the next thing you know you've affected the lives of thousands of people."

"Beautifully stated," said Mary-Armour, "and very lofty to boot. But if you want me to understand what you're driving at, you'll have to be specific."

"All right," I said, "let's take the case of old Grommet. You remember Grommet—he was the one . . ."

Before I could finish, we heard a child's cry from the back of the house.

"A Life Force has been triggered," Mary-Armour said. She got up and started toward the baby's room. Cleopatra, who had gone back to snoozing in front of the fire, wakened, and with all the grace of an aged camel, rose and lumbered down the hall after Mary-Armour. I laced my hands together behind my head and leaned back and shut my eyes, seeing once more that blistering July afternoon when J. B. Grommet and I triggered the Life Forces in each other.

The place was a dusty country grocery store halfway up the Napa Valley in Northern California. The time, according to my waterproof, shockproof, accuracy-resistant U. S. Navy wrist watch, was one-thirty-three, Pacific Daylight Time. An aged Nehi thermometer tacked above the store's gritty front stoop registered 106. The wind velocity was indisputably zero.

I walked through the swinging screen doors, past the

3

barrel filled with brooms, mops, and rake handles, past the homemade island covered with breakfast cereal and blue chambray shirts, past the shelves of canned peas and canned corn and canned peaches, past the fifty-pound sacks of dog food, grass seed, and fertilizer, back to a point deep within the dark cavernous building where a stony-faced brontosaurus of a storekeeper stood with folded arms behind a glassed-in meat counter. As I approached him, walking down the long narrow aisle of his empty store, it seemed possible—indeed, highly probable—that this grocer and I were the only people alive in the entire world.

I came to a halt in front of the meat cabinet. Momentarily I forgot the torrent of perspiration that was coursing down my back, washing rich alluvial deposits of Napa County soil to a fertile delta at the base of my spine. I bared my teeth in a large-economy-size toothpaste smile.

"Good afternoon, Mr. Grommet," I said.

I'd never met the gentleman before, but I knew it was old Grommet, all right. The sign outside said J. B. GROMMET GROCERY & GENERAL STORE, and no mere employee could have given me that authentic I-eat-salesmen-raw-dipped-in-salt look.

Grommet replied to my greeting with a throaty noise that sounded as though he were crushing rocks with his larynx. He was a fat, perspiring man of about fifty, whose complete absence of cranial hair was compensated by a profuse bristly growth that sprouted from his ears, nose, and eyebrows.

"My name is Jim Nelson," I continued.

Old Grommet took this news very calmly. He frowned and bared his right canine incisor.

Looking back on it, of course, I was a fool to have expected any other kind of reception. One look at my blue tropical-worsted suit—I was trying my innocent best to

4

look respectable—established me as an outlander, up to no good. I compounded the error by wearing a hat, and worse yet, a necktie. Grommet, accustomed to salesmen in sport shirts and customers in jeans, must have thought I'd come from another planet.

My worst sin, however, was mechanical, not sartorial. For clutched in my left arm I carried a large, red, squarish penny-gum machine.

"I represent the Multivend Company, Mr. Grommet," I said.

"The what?" Grommet growled.

"The Multivend Company," I said. "We offer a service which I know will please you and your customers. We operate the finest route of penny-gum machines in California."

Grommet made a face as though he smelled sewer gas. He inserted his little finger into his left ear until it nearly went out of sight, and rotated his wrist vigorously.

"Our service," I continued, "involves no cash outlay on your part, naturally. We provide both the machine and the merchandise. And you get a generous—a *very* generous —percentage of the machine's monthly sales."

As Grommet's finger came out of his ear, I heard a faint pop, as though someone had uncorked a bottle.

"What machine?" Grommet said.

"The penny-gum machine I want to install in your store," I said.

"You ain't puttin' no goddam machine in here," he said.

"Of course not," I said soothingly. "Not unless you *want* it. And why should you want it when I haven't explained the many ways my machine can help you, such as—"

"What's your name again? Nielsen?"

"Nelson," I said.

Grommet scowled, "That's what I thought," he said. He

opened his meat cabinet and sliced a generous hunk off a gray wad of Swiss cheese. He put half of it in his mouth and began to chew noisily.

"Now, what we do," I said, "is to put a machine in your store and keep it serviced and looking nice—"

"They was a Nielsen wanted around here for car-stealin', two, three months back," Grommet announced.

"I'm *Nelson*," I said.

"Stole a Buick," Grommet said, staring at me through narrowed eyes. "Up Calistoga way."

I set the gum machine down on the meat cabinet.

"My name," I said slowly, "is Jim Nelson. N-e-l-s-o-n." I felt as though I'd better start all over. "I represent the—"

" 'Bout your height, too," Grommet said, "according to the police circular."

I smiled stiffly. There was no use proceeding until Grommet made up his mind whether or not to phone the sheriff. After a minute of silence, during which Grommet made no move, I decided to plow in again.

"Once a month," I said, "we take the pennies out of the machine and—"

"Car wasn't old either," Grommet said. "Only eight thousand miles."

I nodded up and down and made a silent "o" with my mouth. Grommet hacked off another piece of cheese and wadded it into his mouth. I kept up the nodding routine for a while, giving him his chance to say—if he wanted to— that a car ain't hardly broke in good by eight thousand miles yet. But he didn't. He was too busy licking his fingers and wiping them on his grimy apron. I plugged my smile in once more and turned up the candlepower.

"Your share is twenty per cent of the gross," I said. "And believe me, this merchandise *moves!* When you think that all you have to do is—"

"Eight thousand ain't much mileage for a car nowadays, Nielsen," Grommet said.

"I'm aware of that, Mr. Grommet," I said, a trifle more sharply than I intended.

"Why," Grommet said, "that car was nearly brand-new!"

I inhaled a deep breath and let it out slowly. I folded my arms and stared into Grommet's tiny gray eyes. They were milky and opaque, like cheap marbles. He opened the meat cabinet again, cut a thin slice of salami, removed and dropped the cellophane skin onto the floor, and popped the remainder into his mouth. The odor of garlic hung in the heat-heavy air.

"Well, what's on your mind, Nielsen?" Grommet said suddenly. "Make it fast. I'm a busy man."

"All I want to do," I said briskly, "is to install one machine in your store. Completely at my risk. You get twenty per cent of—"

"Gawdamighty!" Grommet exploded. "Did I say that was a Buick? Must be losin' my mind! It was a Shivvy!"

A drop of perspiration slid from my eyebrow to my glasses and washed down the lens, giving Grommet an undulating, watery look, as though he were at the bottom of the sea. Momentarily I pictured him on the ocean floor, tied in a sack with plenty of rocks.

"Mr. Grommet," I said quietly, "I'm trying to explain my deal to you. You're making it very difficult."

Grommet's shrubby eyebrows shot up innocently. I thought for a moment I saw a wicked flicker of a smile flicker across his face.

"Me?" he said. "Difficult? I don't get you. All you gotta do is talk, son, and I'll sure as hell listen."

With considerable effort, I caused the corners of my mouth to rise. "Fair enough," I said. "All right, here's the deal in a nutshell. I put the machine in. I service it. Once a month I pay—"

Grommet had turned and was starting to walk through a narrow door into his back storeroom.

"Mr. Grommet!" I said.

7

Grommet kept on going. Over his shoulder he said, "Yeah?" Then he disappeared.

For a moment I stood there, dazed. Then I picked up my gum machine, slipped around the end of the meat cabinet, and started after him. I found him leaning against an eight-foot stack of Kleenex cartons, lighting a cigarette. I looked around me. The whole storeroom seemed to be filled with Kleenex. Only in the extreme rear of the room did I see anything else; in one back corner were several tipsy stacks of canned goods and beside them, a topless cardboard box in which a black mother cat nursed a litter of variegated kittens. The other rear corner of the room had been partitioned off with two-by-fours and heavy wallboard to make a tiny, windowless room. A crudely lettered sign on the door to this cubicle read: LAVVATORY. When Grommet saw that I had followed him, he grunted and headed for this door.

"Just a minute, Grommet," I said testily, "I'm trying to talk to you!"

Grommet paused in front of the door and extracted a large doorkey from the pocket of his apron.

"Gotta keep the damn thing locked alla time," he said, "or some of them grape pickers slip back here and use it."

He inserted the key and turned it one revolution counterclockwise. Leaving the key in the lock, he opened the door. Then, with a smug look in my direction, he stepped inside and shut the door.

My self-control was ebbing fast. "Now you listen here!" I shouted. "Just give me a civil answer—that's all I ask! Now, do I put a machine in or not?"

"Hell, no, you don't!" Grommet shouted back. "Jee-zus God! Can't a man have no goddam privacy nowhere?"

Suddenly, staring angrily at the lavatory door, I felt the Life Force triggered within me. I put my hand on the key to the closed door and turned it firmly, one revolution, clockwise.

"Hey!" Grommet said. "What'd you do?" He rattled the door handle.

"You wanted privacy," I said calmly. "Okay, you got it."

I removed the key from the lock, walked across the room to the cat's box, and dropped it in. Then, while Grommet kicked and shouted bloody murder, I walked out of the crowded storeroom, out through the hot, empty store, out into the big, baking, somnolent Napa Valley.

The brilliant sun hit me like a heavy weight, and I blinked. I walked over to my Jeep station wagon, opened the door, and tossed the gum machine onto the dusty rear seat. For a minute I stood motionless, staring at it as though I'd never seen a gum machine before.

I shook my head, to clear it. This is not me, I told myself. The Jim Nelson I used to know was more or less decent, almost respectable; he lived in New York, had a family and a job. He would never lock a man in his own washroom!

Slowly I turned around, mounted the board porch, and pushed once again through the swinging doors of Grommet's grocery. As I neared the back of the store I heard Grommet's voice.

"Nielsen! Help! Anybody!"

The sound was very faint. The giant overpurchase of Kleenex muffled it nicely.

I walked to the wall refrigerator, opened the door, and took out one can of beer. I laid one silver quarter on the white marble till of Grommet's ancient cash register. Then I returned to the Jeep where I shed my hat and coat, loosened my tie, removed an opener from the glove compartment, and punctured the beer can.

As the healing liquid sloshed down my parched throat, I began to feel vaguely repentant. Finally, after I had finished the beer, I entered Grommet's store for the third time. I walked directly to the storeroom, retrieved the key from the cat's box, and approached the washroom door.

"Who's that?" Grommet said anxiously. "Whoever you are, get me out of here!"

"It's me, Grommet," I said. "Nielsen. Will this key fit under that door all right?"

"Sure thing, Nielsen!" Grommet said eagerly. "You just push her under!"

The idea of having J. B. Grommet emerge from his cage while I was still there, however, had little appeal. "Tell you what I'll do," I said. "You have a roll of john paper in there, don't you?"

Grommet paused before answering.

"Yeah," he said warily. "Why?"

"You just start unrolling it," I said, "and pass the free end under the door to me."

"What for?"

"If you want out," I said, "start unrolling."

A piece of white paper peeped out from beneath the door. I picked it up and began slowly to back away.

"Keep it coming," I said, "and don't let it break, or you're finished."

In a very short time there was a long strip of toilet paper extending from the washroom door all the way across the storeroom.

"Okay, that's enough," I said. "Now listen carefully, Grommet. I'm putting the key on the sheet farthest away from you, see? All you have to do is wind the john paper back in, and you'll pull the key under the door in no time. But don't go too fast, or you'll jerk the paper out from under the key. Okay?"

We needn't concern ourselves here with Grommet's blasphemous reply. Suffice it to say that as I left the storeroom, the long strip of paper was moving across the floor with infinite slowness.

Outside once again, I climbed into the Jeep and started the motor. As I pulled out onto the highway, I began wistfully to review the countless primroses that lay along the path from respectability in midtown Manhattan to the recent imbroglio on the dusty boards of J. B. Grommet's Grocery & General Store.

A sudden rush of images brought a lump to my throat —the cozy apartment we'd left just ten months before, on East Fifty-third Street; friends, family, a pleasant job—all left behind. And the city of New York itself. We'd really loved it, Mary-Armour and I.

But if we'd loved all these things so much, why had we left?

I pulled the Jeep to a halt under a large walnut tree beside the road. I turned off the engine and stared out the window at the shimmering waves of heat rising from the black pavement.

Why had we left—it was a good question.

Another picture flashed into my mind—Doctors' Hospital, New York—early morning—a tiny baby, barely an hour old, peering up at me skeptically through the nursery window.

Was Jamie a clue? In a way, I supposed he was. For by the time he was three months old, Mary-Armour and I had already begun to worry about his playing stickball between two sewer lids in Fifty-third Street. Was that any life for Our Boy? Did we want him to grow up knowing only cement and asphalt and dogs on leashes and smog and sootfall and trees with little wire fences around them? No, by George! That boy was going to grow up in the country!

It's quite possible, of course, that Jamie was merely an excuse for his parents to fulfill a wish-dream of their own, because we could have solved our problem quite handily by moving to Long Island, Connecticut, Westchester, or New Jersey, where there was still plenty of Nature—open fields, hand pumps, septic tanks, deer in the garden, poison ivy, and all the rest. But that wasn't what our dream called for. Our dream called for California. Nothing else would do.

You see, in California—we had this on very good authority—the sun was always shining. Everyone lived outdoors, playing croquet and badminton and cooking steaks over open fires. In fact, the only reason a person ever entered a house was that he'd forgot the barbecue sauce.

By the time Jamie was six months old, our dream had become so overpowering that Mary-Armour and I decided the only course open to us was to give in gracefully. A few phone calls later, we had the first of an eager procession of moving-van estimators stumbling through the apartment, counting chairs and trying to guess the weight of our venerable upright piano.

"Do you know how much they want for taking our things to California?" Mary-Armour asked me the next night, after she had entertained the moving fraternity off and on all day.

"How much?" I asked.

"Eleven hundred and fifteen dollars!"

"Jee-rusalem!" I gasped. "Eleven hundred bucks!"

"They're out of their minds!" Mary-Armour said.

A few hours later, as we were getting ready for bed, Mary-Armour asked me how much trucks cost.

"Depends," I said. "What kind of truck?"

"One big enough to haul our furniture to California," she said.

I clapped a hand to my forehead. "Now who's out of whose mind?" I said.

The fact of the matter was, however, that the more I thought about it, the more reasonable the idea began to sound. In fact, it sounded terrific! Auto and truck prices—because of the freight from the factories—had always been higher on the West Coast than the East. If we made a shrewd purchase, we might even sell the truck in California for more than the purchase price in New York! By golly, instead of it costing us eleven hundred dollars to get our belongings across the country, we'd *make* money!

It didn't take us long to case the local truck market and lose our hearts to a large, friendly red truck made by the White Motor Company. My carpentry and Mary-Armour's needlework—both poor but adequate—soon built a wood-canvas-and-foam-rubber bunk for Jamie on the large shelf behind the driver's seat. Now nothing remained but to load the truck—the Van Ordinaire, we had dubbed it— with three tons of child and chattels, and climb aboard.

When the day of departure finally came, we weren't at all sure we still wanted to go. The die had been cast, how-ever, many weeks before and we had no choice now. There-fore we bade a regretful—even tearful—farewell to job, friends, family, and to our beloved New York, and set out for the West.

Our destination was vague: "the area around San Fran-cisco." We wanted to be close enough to this magnificent city to take advantage of its urban civilization, and far enough away to go barefoot.

A more astute husband and father might have found a job for himself before moving his family three thousand truckline miles from one ocean to the other. A wiser man might have gone ahead to prepare the way, to line up the perfect deal.

I claim to be neither wise nor astute. All I know is that somewhere deep down inside me—and inside Mary-Ar-mour, too—there was a feeling that if we waited for the perfect deal to come along, we might end up with no deal at all.

2

Despite the dire—and on the whole, very reasonable—prediction of our neighborhood bookie, who was offering eight-to-five against our getting past Ohio, we finally reached the western Nevada border and began our climb, up over the Sierras into the Promised Land of California.

The trip across the country had taken us a mere nineteen action-packed, thrill-studded days. Let me urge you to follow in our footsteps some time. For if you've never come down the twisting west side of Donner Pass in seven tons of thundering truck, with your wife at the wheel trying vainly to double-clutch into second gear—Buster, you haven't lived!

We holed up temporarily with some hospitable friends in Marin County, just north of San Francisco, and presently moved in on some equally hospitable relatives nearby. We were now, as the movie folk are reputed to say, "on location," and it was up to me to seek some form of gainful employment.

During our first week with Mary-Armour's relatives, I lay in the sun most of the day (our California friends were right—the state did have one hell of a lot of sunshine!) and pondered my next move. My greatest exertion during this trying period was to run my index finger down the columns of Help-Wanted ads, looking for A Position.

Mary-Armour helped. After I'd called it quits and settled down for a snooze, making a tent over my face with the classified, she would pick the paper up, exposing my now-peeling nose to the sun once more, and read the ads herself—out loud.

"Here's one," she said. "Listen: 'Yng. man, some selling exp., five days, $75.' How does that sound?"

I groaned and turned over on my side.

"Okay," she said, "then listen to this one. 'Salesman, must have new-model car. Small investment required.' "

"Look," I said, "I saw that one. I read the ads. So let's give up for today—hmmm? Incidentally, what's Cousin Aggie having for supper?"

And thus another day's work was over.

I like to think that it was only natural for Mary-Armour and me finally to let our eyes wander from the Help-Wanted columns of the newspapers over into the Business-Opportunities department. Business Opportunities, in case you've never spent a lazy Sunday afternoon with the classified, dreaming yourself in and out of a dozen incredibly profitable deals, is a listing of motels, restaurants, gas stations, bars, groceries, and other entrepreneurial ventures which are perpetually on the block.

On a warm Sunday morning, while Jamie crawled around our hosts' garden and ate dirt, Mary-Armour and I spread out the Business Opportunities on the grass, put our heads together, and window-shopped for a business.

"Get this motel deal," I said, pointing to an ad that had caught my interest. "I'd like a motel."

"Perish forbid that I should become a chambermaid," Mary-Armour said.

"This one's in Arizona," I said. "I can see it now, with a lot of sagebrush, and a swimming pool. Did you ever see a play called *The Petrified Forest?*"

"With a motel you're tied down every minute of your life," Mary-Armour said. "You can never leave."

"It ought to be a bargain," I said. "Look, it says 'illness forces sale.' "

"That means the owner is worried sick because the business is going broke."

"Okay, wise guy," I said. "Well, here's one for sale for a different reason—'other interests.' "

"That also means the owner is worried sick about going broke," Mary-Armour said.

I looked up at her sideways. "Say, you're hard as nails this morning, aren't you?"

"Now this toy store in Mill Valley," Mary-Armour said, "that's different. That sounds more like the real thing."

"Nobody ever got rich running a toy store," I said.

"So who wants to get rich?" Mary-Armour asked. "I thought our aim was to enjoy life."

"Well, that's right," I said. "But all I meant was that running a toy store seems so sort of . . . pedestrian. It lacks imagination."

"That doesn't sound like you," Mary-Armour said. "Ordinarily you can inject more imagination into the classified section of a newspaper than anyone I ever heard of."

There was a grain of truth in what she said, because to me there is nothing more romantic and exciting than those little, squashed-up, small-type classified ads. I can't ever remember a time in my life when I didn't pore over them. In first grade I moved directly from my primer to a weekly reading of the *Let's Swap* column ("Trade litter

16

of purebred half-Collie pups for good deer rifle, washing machine, or what?"). It was a habit I never tried to shake, and now Mary-Armour had it too.

"What would you think of running a supermarket?" Mary-Armour asked. I was now lying on my back, watching Jamie gnaw at a dahlia stalk, but Mary-Armour was still hunched over the paper. "Here's one they're giving away free. Listen: 'Sacrifice, $56,000, plus inventory.' "

"Nobody ever just sells anything any more," I said. "They always sacrifice it." I rolled onto my stomach beside her again and picked up reading where I'd left off. And then, without even knowing I was speaking, I said, "Hey!"

"I saw it," Mary-Armour said.

"I mean this one: 'Automat. Vending Machines.' "

"I know."

For a while we were both silent, while we read and reread the ad. It went like this, and I quote:

AUTOMAT. VENDING MACHINES

OWN YOUR
OWN BUSINESS

Whether you start on a small or large scale, there's a plan to fit your needs. Cigarettes, candy, gum and salted nut routes are all set up for you. Just take over and start making profits the first day!

See what vending machines can do for YOU!

Cash Investment	Working hrs. per wk.	Net up to wkly.
$ 500	4 hrs.	$ 50
$ 750	6 hrs.	$ 75
$1,000	8 hrs.	$100
$2,500	20 hrs.	$250
$5,000	40 hrs.	$500

As though that one weren't enough to make you paw at your checkbook, there was another ad further down the page which offered an investment-to-earnings ratio that made the first ad look like downright hard work. It cut the investment one-fifth, sliced the arduous four-hour work stint in half, and offered the same weekly net. It looked like this:

Cash Investment	Working hrs. per wk.	Net up to wkly.
$ 395	2 hrs.	$ 50
$ 795	4 hrs.	$ 90
$1,595	6 hrs.	$180

"Imagine that!" I said to Mary-Armour. "Six hours' work, a hundred and eighty bucks!"

"May I borrow your pencil?" Mary-Armour asked. She began figuring in the margin of the newspaper. While she figured, I crossed the lawn and removed from the tiny pink hands of Master Jamie a rusty knife blade he had found on the lawn and with which he was attempting to disembowel himself.

"Eight times three is twenty-four," Mary-Armour was saying, as I sat back down again, "and seven makes thirty-one. There!"

"Where?"

"I just figured out the annual rate of return on an investment in one of these deals," Mary-Armour said.

"And how much is it?"

"Six hundred and eighty-five per cent!"

"Wow!" I said.

"Wow is right."

"Well," I said, "all I can say is, it makes our Standard Oil look pretty sick."

Mary-Armour raised her eyebrows and touched the end of her nose with the pencil eraser.

"Don't forget, darling," she said, "that Standard Oil is not dealing in such outrageously profitable items as cigarettes, candy, gum, and salted nuts!"

We both realized, of course, that the claims in the ad must have been greatly exaggerated. Still, we couldn't get the idea out of our minds.

"Suppose you had to work twice as long as they say," I said to Mary-Armour that night, as we were getting ready for bed, "and only got half what they promise. Twelve hours work and only ninety bucks a week. It's still not bad, you know."

"It would be nice for you to be your own boss," Mary Armour said.

"Think of that free time," I said. "Suppose I worked only two or three days a week and brought in ninety, a hundred, a hundred and a quarter, something like that. Think of all the things we could do with our spare time."

Mary-Armour nodded and continued to brush her blond hair with long straight strokes.

"I saw a loom advertised in 'Miscellaneous,' " I said.

"I could use a tweed suit," Mary-Armour said.

"There was an electric kiln advertised, too," I said.

"Make the tweed suit for me first, darling," Mary-Armour said, "before you give me feet of clay."

I thought about the loom and the kiln and went to bed with delicious visions before my eyes.

You see, one of our problems in New York had been that we never had time to do all the things we wanted. For one thing, my job took quite a bit of time—I liked it a lot, you understand, but it was a real time-consumer.

Therefore, there was never time left over to make pottery, take jazz piano lessons, write short stories, read *War and Peace*, tinker with automobiles, invent gadgets that needed inventing, dye batik fabrics, play golf, study radio, garden, or do any of a million other things that we felt really should be done.

The more we thought about vending machines, the more it began to look as though we might have stumbled on the answer to all our problems. The operation of vending machines, unless you were abnormally greedy, was obviously a part-time business. True, a certain amount of capital was required to get started, probably more than the optimistic newspaper ads led one to believe, but didn't we have a big expensive truck, just waiting to be converted into cash? And couldn't we make a transfusion from our savings, if necessary, too?

Of course we could! And then, once our route of machines was established, and I was on my two-or-three-days-a-week schedule, Mary-Armour and I would find we had time for all the extracurricular pursuits in the world!

Our first step toward this millennium was to send off a batch of letters, answering each and every vending-machine ad in the San Francisco Sunday papers. The fact that there were a good many of them gave us no pause, although we did notice one thing that made us wonder: about 90 per cent of the ads were blind—that is, they gave newspaper box numbers to reply to, rather than their street addresses and telephone numbers. Being faintly less naïve than you have a right to imagine, we got the impression that perhaps some of these advertisers might be a bit on the fly-by-night side.

While we waited for mail replies, I got on the bus and rode into San Francisco to call on the No-Name Vending Machine Company, the one firm that had given a street address. I did my best to look worldly and sophisticated as I walked in No-Name's unpretentious front door. I wore my best suit, and what I hoped was a look of skepticism. Backing me up I had four years of college, five years on a savvy business magazine, and a pock-marked savings account. I told myself that I was a well-heeled man of the world. No San Francisco slicker was going to put anything over on me, no sir!

And yet, somehow, the people at No-Name saw hay wisps sticking out of my hat.

I had expected an immediate blast of high pressure, so I was quite surprised to find everything at No-Name very folksy and exaggeratedly unfurbished. Since I saw no one in the front display area, I walked directly to a starkly simple glassed-in office at the rear of the floor. Some gold leaf on the door proclaimed: "Truslow Thomas, Pres." I knocked politely, then opened the door and stuck my head in.

"I want to talk to someone about vending machines," I said.

Truslow Thomas was on his feet immediately. "Of course," he said soothingly, extending his hand. I shook it warily, introducing myself, and tried to take his measure. He was tall and cadaverous; his skin looked to be made of wax. His cheeks and temples were remarkably concave, and his huge dark eyes were set far back in his head, beneath thick, shaggy brows. His bony cranium was crowned with an impressive thatch of wavy black hair that sprang straight up from his waxy forehead. His manner expressed an infinite and mysterious sadness. He arched his luxuriant eyebrows.

"A pleasure, Mr. Nelson," he said sadly, thoughtfully. "Take a chair." The arched eyebrows flattened, dipped, rose again. They were constantly on the move, seeming to express a whole barrelful of delicate emotions—joy that I had come, concern lest my chair was too hard, eagerness to help me in any way, and lastly, when I explained my modest desire to earn an easy, part-time hundred dollars a week, sympathetic understanding.

"Of course, of course," Thomas said, in a tone of voice customarily reserved for the bereaved. "Naturally." Then his face changed. An expression of mild happiness crossed it, the thin lips framed a smile. Finally, like a theater curtain going up, the eyebrows lifted, and for a moment the look of sorrow left the eyes.

"You've come to the right place, Mr. Nelson," he said. I saw now that his momentary happiness came from the fact that he was going to be able to help me. He walked to the office door, stuck his head out, and intoned sonorously:

"Mr. Chugwater, please."

The genial Humpty-Dumpty who rolled into his office as though on ball bearings was the complete opposite of Truslow. He was immense, baby-pink, and very nearly spherical. His face was completely unlined, and he wore a pair of bifocals, one bow of which had been mended with adhesive tape. His suit, a bold brown-and-orange check, had apparently been purchased during an earlier, thinner era. He was equipped with an enormous amount of personal hardware, including a jewel-tipped collar-pin which was attached to one collar tab and reached vainly for the other. His cuff-links were large and ornate and depicted the head of a very angry stallion in bas-relief. On his left wrist he wore a silver watchband, and on his right, a matching silver identification bracelet. A gold chain meandered like a transcontinental railroad across his broad expanse of vest. From it dangled two or three unidentified keys (one looked like a Phi Beta Kappa, and wasn't) and a large yellow tooth, perhaps his own. Below the vest were two or three inches of exposed shirt and then, marking his equator, a large hand-wrought copper belt buckle. He wore two rings on his left hand, one of plain gold, the other a tiny diamond chip mounted in an impressively large setting, and on his right hand he wore a massive class ring of the kind worn by graduates of West Point, Annapolis, and most U.S. high schools.

There was no hint of sadness about Chugwater. For the moment he radiated only one emotion, good cheer, and that by the bucketful.

"Rightee-oh, Truss," he said. His voice crackled with good fellowship. He beamed a friendly smile in my direction and then looked expectantly toward Truslow Thomas.

"This is our man in charge of route-building," Thomas told me. Thomas' eyebrows seemed to be stuck temporarily in the upward, or joy, position. "Mr. Ogden Chugwater. Og, meet up with Jim Nelson."

Og extended his puffy right paw, and I discovered that it contained neither bone nor muscle.

"Mr. Nelson wants to learn the facts about our machines," Thomas said.

"Splendid, splendid!" Chugwater burbled, rubbing his hands together. "How about lunch, Jim? Be my guest!"

On the way out of No-Name, Chugwater punched the cash register and extracted a ten-dollar bill.

"Forgot my wallet today," he explained cordially, looking over his shoulder toward Thomas' door.

In a drafty restaurant nearby, a basement job with murals of half-naked Valkyries on three walls, and what Og called "an unparalleled nude" over the bar (how can a nude remain unparalleled for long?), we sat down at a small table and ordered wiener-schnitzel sandwiches, the specialty of the house. While we were waiting, Og set a new speed record for the three-martini freestyle, urging me to come on in, because the water, or whatever it was they put in them, was fine. Because I was trying to keep my head clear for business, however, I abstained.

"The first thing you've got to remember about vending machines, Jim," Chugwater told me confidentially after we had kissed off the weather and similar small talk, "is that the woods are full of sharpies—shysters who would just as soon rob you as look at you."

"I rather suspected as much, Mr. Chugwater," I said, smiling shrewdly.

"Og," he said. "Call me Og."

"Thank you, Og," I said. How could anyone withstand such earnest good intentions?

"Those sharpies make the *most* outrageous claims!" Og snorted. "Maybe you've seen some of them—simply outrageous! Why, who ever heard of a man making fifty bucks a week on an investment of $500? And four hours work!" He waved his jeweled hand grandly, at the same time signaling the waiter. "Impossible!" he said.

"I told my wife those ads were over-optimistic," I said, almost believing that I had.

The waiter arrived with a fourth martini. Og did a perfect back-jackknife into it and came up with the lemon peel in his teeth.

"Those birds ought to be in jail!" he said fervently.

For several minutes Og and I sat in silent communion, knitted closer by our common bond of outrage. Then, the atmosphere changed suddenly. Over the wiener schnitzel, Og discovered that he and I had both lived in New York. Ah, New York! Og had touched a sensitive nerve. Eating places—Og reminisced about his favorites while I waited to get a word in about mine. The Lexington Avenue subway—what a rat-race at rush hour! Ah, those crazy taxi drivers—what characters, especially on rainy days!

We didn't talk much more during lunch about gum merchandising, or about the kind of deal No-Name generally made, or about what it cost to get set up in business. The closest we came was late in the meal when Og began wistfully to tell me about the route of machines he hoped to have in a few years when he was ready to retire.

"It's just going to be a modest little route," he told me. I could see the misty, faraway look in his watery, little eyes and hear the music of coins jingling in his pockets. "Not enough machines to make me work more than a day or two a week," he said, "but just enough to keep me comfortably fixed for the rest of my life."

For a brief instant I wondered why, if vending-machine routes were so profitable, Og didn't kick over the traces at No-Name and set himself up for The Good Life right away. The thought passed all too quickly.

After lunch we went back to No-Name and looked at machines. Og showed me how simple they were to service, how easy to install anywhere, even on a concrete wall. The operating mechanism, he told me, was foolproof. To prove it, he handed me the key to a shiny red machine loaded with peanuts.

"Here," he said. "You try it."

I unlocked the front of the machine. The door swung open easily. I pushed and pulled all the movable parts.

"That's the locking lever," Og said. "That's the merchandise wheel, that's the vending cup . . ." Everything operated with the precision of a Swiss watch. (I had not yet heard of "the worker"; see page 51.) I locked the machine finally and handed the keys to Og.

He handed me a penny. "Try it," he said.

I inserted the penny in the coin slot, turned the handle, and received an enormous handful of fresh, salted nuts. While I munched on them contentedly, Og opened the machine, retrieved his penny, and motioned for me to follow him to his barren office.

Seating himself at his scarred desk, he reached into his bottom left-hand drawer and pulled out a dogeared sheet of accounting paper which purported to show the earnings of a salted-nut route somewhere in the central valley of California. I was so smitten by the names of the places where the machines were located (The Coco Palms, The

Seven Seas, Grandma's, The Hunky-Dory, etc.) that I wasn't able to follow the figures exactly. I did gather, however, that the lucky operator of this route was pulling in a net that averaged just over one dollar per machine per week. Og assured me that this was the case. It was No-Name's guarantee (what qualifying word he said under his breath, I didn't catch) that a properly located machine—and who could locate them more properly than No-Name—would net at least one buck per week.

It didn't take me long to figure out that if I wanted to rough it on $100 a week while I wove tweed suits and tried my hand at mosaics, I would have to have 100 machines.

Og was a little vague on exactly how much it would cost to put 100 machines in the field, but I gathered I would have to shell out something in the neighborhood of $5,000. This was considerably more than I'd had in mind to spend. In fact, before my session with Og, the idea of shelling out five thousand cherished one-dollar bills for any business short of Gimbel's would have paralyzed me. But now that Og had made everything so clear . . . why, if I netted $100 a week—as I was nearly practically almost absolutely certain of doing—the whole shooting match would pay for itself inside a year!

Just before I caught the bus back to Marin County, Og told me a little parable to illustrate how difficult it was for a novice to place machines on location—just in case that idea had occurred to me. The parable concerned a man in Grampus, Idaho, a man who had lived in Grampus so many years that he knew everyone. I mean *everyone!* What's more, this man was exceedingly well liked. He was so well liked, in fact, that he decided he didn't need the services of No-Name in placing a batch of machines on location. Cocky soul that he was, he just had No-Name ship him the machines so he could put them on location himself, and thus save the cost of having No-Name do it for him.

Once the machines got there, however, the man found he could hardly persuade anyone to let him install one. Even his oldest friends found excuses to explain why he couldn't put machines in their stores and restaurants.

In the end, of course, the poor misguided soul had to wire No-Name to come out and do the job for him after all. Which No-Name was glad to do, naturally—no grudges at No-Name—and the old boy immediately got very rich and lived happily ever after, amen.

Somehow the idea of me placing my own machines on location had never occurred to me until Og told his story. I told Og he'd just posed an interesting possibility, and I asked him how much less the machines would cost if I did my own locating.

For a moment I thought perhaps Og had choked on a cashew. His pink face grew deep red, and he gasped and coughed for a few moments, but when he finally recovered, he gave me a rather long-winded, vague answer, the logic of which was rather hard to follow. What it all boiled down to, however, was that the machines would still cost about $5,000. The locating cost was really extremely small, Og said, and, begging my pardon, a tyro like me probably couldn't locate a machine in my own closet.

I felt quite enthusiastic about gum machines as I rode the bus home that night, loaded with pamphlets that described No-Name's machines in suitably glowing terms. Mary-Armour read each brochure from beginning to end and asked a lot of questions I couldn't answer. She wasn't quite as enthusiastic as I, but I knew that would come in time. Meantime I promised to ask Og her questions the next time I went into the city.

The following evening, Tony Barloff of National Western Automatic, Inc., telephoned in answer to one of my letters. His voice was vibrant with urgency. He wanted to come over and talk to me right away. He hoped that the little woman (his words, not mine) would be there. He explained that it would be better for him to come to me than vice versa, because his office was far, far away, off in the distant reaches of Oakland.

Tony arrived half an hour later in a white-walled hard-top convertible. He was a well-sandpapered article about twenty-five, with clear blue eyes and elaborately waved blond hair. His clothes looked expensive, if somewhat zooty, and his calling card was made of red celluloid printed with gold letters. Under his arm he carried a leather-bound notebook filled with pictures of various types of vending machines, and data on how rich you could get, how soon, with how many machines.

"My, what a charming place!" Tony said, as he stepped inside the front door. It was a good line, but it sounded as though it had been written for someone else.

Tony's best buy was a coffee-vending machine which he offered, on location and minting money, for something more than $1,200. These machines, he told us, had a tremendous capacity, which meant that the operator hardly ever had to bother servicing them, and even when he did, it only took about five minutes of his time. There was one exception to this, however, and Tony dutifully told us about it.

"Sometimes," he said dramatically, lifting both hands in the air, like a man who had just seen an angel, "a machine just goes wild!"

"Goes wild?" Mary-Armour echoed.

"It takes off," Tony amplified. "It goes crazy. Like this, see. There's a bunch of people working in this factory where you've got your machine. Naturally they drink a lot of coffee—everyone does; it's our number-one national habit. But one afternoon, see, they're working, making washers or something, and for some reason they all get thirsty at once. Maybe it's a cold day, or they all had ham for lunch, or something. Anyhow, they all want coffee, and they want it bad! So they go to your machine, see, and they start putting in dimes, and they keep putting them in and having a second cup and maybe a third, they're so goddam thirsty for coffee, see? Pretty soon, everybody in the plant's doing it, and all of a sudden your machine is practically empty except for the coin box, which is chock full of dimes—maybe a hundred dollars worth, maybe even more!"

My mind reeled. For a minute I thought I could see the angel, too.

"Does this actually happen?" I asked incredulously.

"Happens all the time," Tony said casually. "It's one of the delightful hazards of the coffee-machine business."

The next thing I saw before me was labeled "Contract of Purchase." It was a thing of beauty—a few bold-faced phrases adrift in a sea of small print—but Mary-Armour and I wanted time to think.

"Can we sleep on it?" I asked. For a moment Tony looked genuinely hurt, as though we'd questioned his integrity. Then he brightened.

"I'll call you in a day or so," he said. "But you'd better hustle—the good spots might disappear overnight!"

Later that night when I closed my eyes and dreamed I was a coffee-machine magnate, I could see my machines going wild day after day. Business was so good, in fact, that instead of devoting five minutes apiece to them once a week, I was forced to give each one five minutes of my time *every day of the week*. This I graciously consented to do, naturally, because of the lush profits, although eventually, of course, I found an honest, unemployed man wandering around loose in my dream, and I hired him at a nominal wage to handle the chore for me.

Mary-Armour and I talked coffee machines to each

other a good bit during the next few days, and the more we talked, the better they sounded to both of us. Tony phoned once or twice to dig his spurs into our tender flanks, but even though we were eager, we held him off a while longer.

And then, one day, between calls from Tony, we made up our minds. We were ready. We had thought it all out carefully, and had made our decision. We would be big wheels in the coffee racket. The next time Tony called, we would tell him to bring on the small print.

The next move, of course, was to drop by No-Name and tell them of our decision. Mary-Armour and I both felt we owed them that courtesy since I had accepted Og's hospitality at lunch.

"*Coffee machines!*" Og gasped, his face registering first horror, then pity, then irreversible shock. But finally he composed his features—obviously with difficulty—and spoke more calmly. "Jim," he said, "I'm sorry. I shouldn't let my own personal feelings intrude into your affairs."

"Oh, that's all right," I said. "But I just thought I ought to tell you."

"Of course," Og said. "Very nice of you. Very decent. And if you're not afraid of coffee machines—after all you've probably heard about them—then I admire your courage." He looked sadly out the front window and fingered the tooth on his watch chain. "Ah, youth," he said. "Afraid of nothing."

I frowned. "I don't get that remark about admiring my courage. What did that mean?"

"Nothing, Jim, nothing," Og said, turning toward me. "Forget it. I certainly don't want to knock another man's machine—especially if you've made up your mind. It's even possible that *your* coffee machines might not be like everyone else's. After all, the law of averages should see that *someone* gets a few good machines."

"Og," I said, "tell it to me straight. Is there something

wrong with coffee machines that I don't know about?"

Og pursed his lips. He shook his head. Momentarily, he gave close scrutiny to one of his stud-horse cuff-links. He was obviously trying to keep his feelings in check.

"I shouldn't be talking this way," he said finally. "After all, it's your money. You should be free to squander it any way you want." He looked out the window again. "A free America is a strong America—right?"

"Og, what did you mean by the word, 'squander'?"

"Sorry," he said. "I should have used another word."

"Look, Og," I said, "quit beating around the bush. Say what you mean."

"Jim," Og said, a quavering note of father-to-son creeping into his voice, "there's a million bugs in coffee machines today, boy. I don't know why the manufacturers can't seem to lick 'em, but they can't. Some day they will, Jim—they're bound to. And when they do, that will be the time to get into coffee—it might even turn into a good business. But right now . . ." He shook his head sadly, then looked up as though he had a new thought. "But maybe you'd make out all right anyhow—didn't you tell me you were an electronic engineer?"

"God, no!" I said. "I majored in English Literature. I don't know thing-one about electronics."

"Well . . ." Og looked thoughtful. "Maybe you could hire someone who knows about it, because they're the only ones who can really service coffee machines. You see, they're not simple little trouble-free machines like these." His rings clicked as he patted one of his machines affectionately. "What did this fellow ask for his machine, by the way?"

"Twelve hundred and fifty," I said. "Or thereabouts."

"Good Lord!" Og said. "What kind was it?" I named the make. For a moment he fumbled through some literature on his desk. Then, triumphantly, he came up with it —an advertisement for the very machine Tony Barloff had offered me. The price printed at the bottom of the page was $895, f.o.b., Kansas City.

"We could put that same machine on location for you for under a thousand," Og said, leaning back in his chair and folding his arms behind his head. "But we wouldn't do it, Jim. No, sir. Not till they get the bugs out, so a man can make a little money without having them go on the fritz all the time."

"You wouldn't even handle them?" I said.

Og came forward in his chair. He took off his bifocals, laid them on the desk, and ran his hand thoughtfully through his limp crew cut.

"Jim," he said, shaking his head seriously, "if you laid the cash down on the table and said you wanted a coffee machine, I'd tell you to put it back in your pocket. No, sir, I wouldn't saddle a man with coffee machines when I knew that for the same money we could build him a good, solid, depression-proof gum-and-candy route in less than three weeks from the time we got the down payment!"

3

"Chewing gum," I told Mary-Armour that night, "is a much better deal than coffee. Much better."

"I thought we just spent four days searching our souls and came up with exactly the opposite conclusion," Mary-Armour said.

"Sweetie, gum has coffee licked seventeen ways from Sunday."

"That's not what you told me last night."

"Forget what I told you last night!" I said. "Listen to what I'm telling you now. There are a million bugs in coffee machines—did you know that? No, you didn't. Okay, neither did I, but there are."

"Og says so?"

"Og says so. Og could sell us that same machine for under a thousand, but he won't. He won't even touch a coffee machine till they get the bugs out."

"Morbid fear of bugs?"

"Listen, sweetie, I'm serious!"

"All right," Mary-Armour said. "I'll go along with whatever kind of machine you decide on. There's just one thing—how do we know Og and No-Name are on the up and up?"

Obviously, my wife had never *met* Og, or she wouldn't have been talking like that!

"Well, I suppose we could check with our bank," I said, "although it's nothing more than a formality. No-Name's okay, you can take my word for that."

"Meaning no offense," Mary-Armour said, "I'd just as soon take the bank's."

The bank's report, which we received three days later, was encouraging. Apparently No-Name kept its nose clean in financial circles, for the report showed that they paid their bills promptly; they financed routes for would-be operators through one of the large local banks, and the routes were seldom if ever repossessed. The company had been doing business at the same old stand for twenty-odd years. (On second thought, remove the hyphen from "twenty-odd.")

"Well, kiddo," I said jauntily to Mary-Armour, as we perused the bank's findings, "does that satisfy you, or do you have to know Chugwater's blood type?"

"I'm satisfied," Mary-Armour replied. "Get your magic wand and turn me into a gumball tycoon."

The following Monday, therefore, I hopped a bus and headed for San Francisco, a man with a delicate mission. No Big-Four foreign minister ever approached a quadripartite meeting with more power in his brief case than I. My government had given me *carte blanche* to negotiate, on arrival, whatever deal seemed best to my trained mind.

There were two chief decisions to be made. One was to decide in what part of the California countryside we would have No-Name set our business up; the other was to decide what kind of No-Name machines we would purchase.

No-Name handled two main kinds of venders. One Og referred to as a bulk vender, which meant that in exchange for a penny or a nickel it dispensed a piece of ball bubble gum, or a handful of nuts or tiny, unwrapped candies. No-Name's other money-maker was a tab-gum vender, tab gum being small paper-wrapped pieces of national-brand chewing gum—Dentyne, Juicy Fruit, and the like—all selling for a penny a stick.

Even without my telling him, Og sensed my go-ahead frame of mind. He bubbled over with helpful suggestions. He strongly recommended that a "diversified route" be built, consisting of fifty bulk venders and fifty tab-gum machines. As to the territory, why, there were some wonderful opportunities—I mean opportunities that were truly magnificent—in a number of nearby places. The best spots, Og said, would be the state capital, Sacramento, or a place called Paso Robles. (I, being new to California and proud of having taken Spanish 10, 20, and 30, called it Pah-soe Roe-blays; Og called it Passa Roe-buls.)

Sacramento, I explained to Og, wasn't close enough to San Francisco to fit Mary-Armour's and my pastoral vision of The Good Life; we had to be able to make frequent quick trips to the city to attend the theater, to gape at art exhibits, to take in the symphony, etc. Passa Roebuls was twice as far away.

Og seemed disappointed when I expressed my timid dissatisfaction with the spots he had suggested. He got out a tired roadmap and a rhinestone-studded ball-point and began adding up mileages.

"Sacramento's only ninety miles," he said, tipping his head back and squinting at the map through the bottom of his bifocals. "Good road all the way. It's an easy two hours."

"How about Marin County?" I asked. It was about the

only part of the Bay area I knew. Mary-Armour and I both liked it a lot—it was where we were staying, of course —and it seemed to fill the bill perfectly as to city-proximity, population, and income. In my mind's eye, as Og stared thoughtfully at his roadmap, I began to weave a little picture of Jim Nelson, the Penny-Gum Man, speeding through the Marin towns—Sausalito, Mill Valley, San Anselmo, San Rafael. On my outward trip the car was laden with ball bubble gum. On my return, the springs sagged under the heavy load of pennies. As I pulled into the palm-lined drive, Mary-Armour ran out to meet me, open-armed. Jamie gurgled happily at me from his play-pen. And then suddenly the pennies were miraculously converted to crisp, green twenty-dollar bills, and a baby sitter appeared out of thin air. Smiling benignly, resplendent in our evening clothes and fake jewelry, Mary-Armour and I climbed into the Mercedes and whizzed across the Golden Gate Bridge into San Francisco to attend the opera.

Og's voice punctured my dream. "I've made it in an hour and forty minutes," he said, "but of course the traffic was light. Sacramento's a little warm in summer, but it's not a patch on Fresno or Bakersfield or any of those places!"

"Marin County's cool in the summer," I countered. I had no idea whether I was right or wrong; I merely wanted to bring Chugwater back from his Sacramento reveries. "How about Marin County?" I repeated, a little louder this time.

"Oh, no!" Chugwater said in a shocked tone of voice, hearing me for the first time. "Not Marin County! We've *got* an operator in Marin County!" Og then proceeded to tell me that No-Name gave a franchise with each route it built, and that no matter how much another person might offer, No-Name would rather cut off the right arm of every man in the organization than attempt to build a second route in already franchised territory.

Naturally, I was disappointed. Mary-Armour and I really sort of had our hearts set on Marin County.

I believe Og must have sensed my disappointment, because he changed the subject temporarily and began to spin some new and beautiful fairy tales, stories of the routes he had built and the men he had turned into gumball tycoons overnight. The will to believe is a potent thing indeed, and my will was strong. I smiled happily as he wove the bright fabric of short hours and big profits. I nodded reprovingly over the yarn about the only man who had ever failed at the business, a miserable lush who couldn't stay sober long enough to give his faithful machines the brief weekly ministrations they required. I nearly wept as Og painted a picture of the drunkard's hundred little money-makers sitting empty, while their master caroused in a bar so crummy that no decent operator would install even a penny peanut machine.

"What happened to his route, finally?" I asked.

"Oh, we took it off his hands," Og answered cryptically.

Gumballing at the present time, Og continued, was almost synonymous with science. I sat, rapt, as he described how No-Name's locators, men skilled in the dynamics of picking the right locations for their machines, approached a town. Their first move was to get a supply of street maps. Then they pinpointed the schools. Often they sat for hours in their cars, watching to see where school children crossed the street, where passengers alighted from buses, where foot traffic was high enough to justify placing one or more of the mechanical merchandisers. You and I might miss all the best spots in a town, but not these men. They didn't miss a single one. They knew, these men did, they *knew!*

I don't know who first mentioned Sonoma County, Og

or myself, but somehow, between stanzas of the Gumball Hymn which Chugwater was caroling, I discovered that we were discussing it. Now, Sonoma is the next county north of Marin County, which is just north of San Francisco. Outside of the fact that it wasn't too far from San Francisco, I really knew nothing about it (I hadn't even been there), and neither, I suspect, did Og. But somehow, here we sat, discussing the possibility of establishing a gum route there.

The longer we talked about it, the more intimately acquainted Og became with every fact about the area. As soon as he could find it on his tattered road map, he began extolling the climate, the busy towns, the high percapita income. He ran his finger up and down the map, chuckling appreciatively over the fine prospects.

"Why, there are thousands of good little towns in that county," he chortled. "Thousands! Petaluma, Cotati, Santa Rosa, Sonoma, Fulton, Windsor, Healdsburg, Hopland, Cloverdale . . ."

Chugwater loved the sound of the names, and so did I. I could visualize them as he read them off—tiny cities really, rather than towns—buzzing with activity, thriving, growing, and sadly enough, lacking a place for the population to spend its pennies. Chugwater would have named every town up to the Oregon border, 390 miles away, if I hadn't interrupted him.

"What about competition?" I asked.

"Nil," he answered grandly. "Practically nil."

"The word 'practically,'" I said, "implies that there are *some* machines in the area. What about them?"

Chugwater pointed to the bright, shiny new machine sitting on his desk. "A machine like this," he said, "will knock the competition right out of any location that's worth having."

That was good, I decided, although I felt a little mean, driving those other poor operators out of business.

"Og," I said, "I was all set to sign up today for Marin County, but of course that's already taken. Now, this Sonoma County deal sounds good, but I think I'd like to drive up there some time in the next few days and—you know—take a look at the countryside."

"No need to do that," Og said. "Take my word for it —it's wonderful country."

"I'm sure it is," I said. "I just want my wife to see it, too."

"Well, why not do this then?" Og said, fumbling in his top desk drawer. "You just sign this little agreement— it's nothing really, just shows that we're of the same mind about the route—and we'll start laying the machines out for you, *while* you're looking. No need to lose any time, just because your wife wants to see the country."

"Og," I said, "I don't think I ought . . ."

"You don't want someone else snapping it up right before your eyes, do you?"

"No, but . . ."

"Fellow phoned in from Santa Rosa the other day about a route," Og said.

"Is that right?"

"He seemed pretty interested," Og said.

"Well, I'm interested, too," I said. "Pretty doggone interested! But I'm the guy who's going to have to live in this place we're talking about—maybe for years. And I can't sign up to go live there without taking a look first! I just can't do it!"

"Sure, pal," Og said, his voice suddenly tender, consoling. "I understand. Tell you what. You take a quick look, and I'll see if I can't stave this Santa Rosa fellow off for a while. Okay?"

"Og, you're a prince!" I said. I couldn't have meant it more.

The following day, a cold, rainy day late in November, Mary-Armour and Jamie and I borrowed a car from our genial hosts and drove off to inspect Sonoma County. I drove, and Mary-Armour navigated, and Jamie sat between us in a very handy collapsible car seat that kept collapsing whether you wanted it to or not. It seemed strange not to be driving the truck, and almost sinful to be able to accelerate, going uphill.

The rain rained, and the fog fogged, and on we went, peering out at the moist countryside and, from time to time, extricating our moist son from his sagging car seat to equip him with fresh diapers.

"It doesn't look *too* bad," Mary-Armour said judiciously, as we ate lunch in a roadside restaurant.

"If only it weren't so doggone wet!" I said.

"It'll be nice when the sun comes out," Mary-Armour said. "It'll probably be beautiful—all those fields and orchards."

"Wouldn't it be great to have your own orchard?" I asked.

Mary-Armour looked up, her eyes alight. "Maybe we could rent an old farm or something!" she said. "Jamie would love it!"

The following week I made two more inspection trips. I was looking now, not so much at the countryside as at the number of gum machines already in the area. I didn't want to set up business in an area that already had its share of gum magnates. I searched for competition in Petaluma, Sonoma, and in the neighboring county of Napa, where Og had told me we would probably install some machines. Happily, the number of gum venders was small.

On a beautiful Friday afternoon soon afterward, therefore, I sat down at Og's battered desk and watched as he filled out a purchase order for one hundred machines. When he had finished, he turned it toward me. He handed me his rhinestone-studded ball-point pen as decorously as though I were the British ambassador about to initial a treaty.

Even as callow a person as I, however, reads a contract that calls for him to hand over some $5,000 to another party. On the whole, the contract seemed fairly innocuous until I came to a shocking provision which declared: "In the event suit is brought by either party to enforce this contract, or any provision thereof, the purchaser agrees to pay all costs of suit, including such sum as the Court may adjudge reasonable for attorneys' fees incurred by No-Name Vending Machine Company."

"Og," I said, feeling a certain amount of embarrassment at even mentioning it, "we both know that we're not going to have any litigation over this deal, but in the unlikely event that we do, do you think it's quite fair for me to have to pay your attorneys' fees?"

"Oh, that," Chugwater said deprecatingly. He leaned back in his chair and rotated his identification bracelet around his wrist. "Just a standard provision of all these contracts. Don't you worry, Jim boy, we won't have any trouble."

"Og," I said, "I still don't like it . . ."

"Would you feel better if we just struck that out?" Og asked. Good old Og, I thought; willing to pay his own lawyer! His rings flashed as he crossed out the offending paragraph. "There. How's that?"

I reread the contract, accepted the ball-point pen, and started to write my name. The pen made a deep gully in the paper, but no ink came out. I shook the pen. Still no ink.

Out of the files of memory came that old advertisement of the 1920s, showing a city slicker out in a cornfield selling something—a new car, maybe—to old Silas, the farmer. Si was all worked up over the idea of owning an air-cooled Franklin, but the slicker's fountain pen went dry just as Si was leaning down from the seat of his disk harrow to sign the contract. Then, the ad told us, Si had some second thoughts about the Franklin—after all, the barn needed fixin', and there was still a mortgage on his wife's upper plate—and the slicker lost the sale. The moral of the tale, of course, was pointed at slickers, not at farmers: Buy a Jones Brothers fountain pen, the only fountain pen that won't let you down in a cornfield!

Momentarily I wondered if there was a message in this for me. But before I had a chance to think much about it, Og was leaning over me, blowing out rich fumes of gin and vermouth, pressing another pen into my hand.

I took a last look at the contract. It showed that the route was to cost $5,200, plus a sales tax of $156. On the contract Og had added these two figures together and come up with the final grand total that I would owe— $5,256. I cocked an eyebrow at that, but then I decided there was no reason for one big dealer to call another's attention to so small an error.

I poised my hand over the contract. I started to write my name. I wrote it. Without a whimper. And then, for an encore, I wrote out a check for $2,600 and handed it to Og. I halfway expected No-Name's employees to spring out from the furniture and send up a cheer.

"Let's see, today's December eighth," I said, ticking off the days on my fingers. "I guess I ought to have the route about the first of the year?"

"Don't you worry," Chugwater said. "You'll get your route. We'll get it on location for you just as fast as we can. Of course, the rains may slow us down some—it's hard for a man to work in the rain. And it's pretty near Christmas—that always slows you down because store-keepers are pretty busy this time of year. But don't you worry, boy, don't you worry!"

Do you mind if I drag in one more story, the one about

the man who on Friday asked a colleague to lend him ten dollars until the following Monday?

"Why, sure, Bill," said the colleague, handing over the ten-spot. "Gladly. And you'll pay me back Monday?"

"Stop hounding me!" Bill snapped, walking away haughtily. "You'll get your money!"

Chugwater's you'll-get-your-gumball-route was not haughty—possibly because there was still another $2,-656 to be extracted from me—but my feelings were pretty much the same ones the ten-spot lender must have felt. Nevertheless, I promised Og not to worry and walked out into the bright winter sunshine.

It was a gorgeous day, warm enough in the sun to take a sunbath, cool enough in the shade to make you walk briskly, wishing you had worn a topcoat. I got into my borrowed car and headed for the Golden Gate Bridge. San Francisco was its beautiful best. The air was invigorating, the bridge was an orange poem, Marin was a gray-green dream. Everything was so lovely, in fact, that I immediately broke my promise to Og and began to worry.

4

No-Name gave us plenty of time to worry. Christmas came and went while Mary-Armour and I looked for a house in Sonoma County from which to operate our empire, and in which to paint, invent, write, weave, vegetate, and raise a flock of small children. After much looking we found a pleasant, largish house for rent on five acres in the country. We snapped it up (it cost less than our tiny New York apartment) after noting that it had a spare bedroom up in the branches of an enormous oak tree. This room was completely finished, screened-in, and wired for electricity, and I felt it would be a perfect workshop for the million-and-one projects Mary-Armour and I would soon be conducting in the immense amount of spare time we were going to have.

Having found a house, we bade farewell to our tolerant relatives in Marin County, climbed aboard our truck once again, and started off. Jamie was a little bit larger than when we had left New York, but he still fitted nicely onto the shelf behind the driver's seat.

It was a gloriously sunny day, and it felt good to be riding in our truck once more. Mary-Armour hummed, and Jamie gurgled, and the truck purred like a contented kitten. When we reached our new home, it was a real pleasure to exercise our rusty muscles, moving our belongings out of the truck and stacking them in a big, undigested heap in the living room.

From his playpen, set in the middle of our lusciously green front lawn, Jamie watched us unload. From time to time, as we passed by carrying chairs and lamps, he gave a series of happy little squawks.

"Isn't that sweet," Mary-Armour said. "He's singing!"

It took almost half a day before we finally had the last piece of furniture out of the truck. There was a certain satisfaction in swinging the big back doors closed and locking them for the last time. When I turned around, Mary-Armour threw her arms around my neck and kissed me.

"Thank you very much," I said. "But what was that for?"

"That was because I feel sorry for all the poor girls who married steady, reliable men," she said.

Arms linked, we walked toward the house. Suddenly I blinked—was the bush on the far side of the drive moving? I stopped walking and stared at it.

"What is it?" Mary-Armour asked.

"We are not alone," I said. I called toward the bush. "Hello—who is it?"

A squat, grumpy-looking old man in overalls, blue work shirt, and a broad-brimmed straw hat that was clearly too big for him—it rested on his ears, pushing them down and out like inverted coat hooks—stepped out from behind the bush. I had the feeling he'd been there quite a while.

He chewed quietly on a long straw as he directed his shiny black eyes all around our front yard and then, with an elaborate look of surprise, turned our way.

"Well, I'll be!" he said. "Didn't know you was here! Lost one of my rabbits. Little brown fella. You must be the new folks, eh?"

"That's right," I said.

The stranger frowned and removed his straw hat, displaying an unruly mass of snow-white hair. With his index finger he made a circuit of the hat's sweatband and then wiped his finger on the bib of his overalls. His ears remained in the outspread position, ready to support the hat again at any time.

"Name's Simmons," he said. "Live a few rods down the road. Raise prunes and rabbits. Lived there sixty-two years. Chickens, too."

In return for this somewhat unsorted information, I told Mr. Simmons who we were. After he had wiped his right palm ceremoniously on the seat of his pants, we all shook hands.

"You buy this place?" Simmons asked.

"No, we're renting it," Mary-Armour replied.

"Hell of a place," he said. "Lease, or month to month?"

We both paused before answering.

"Month to month," Mary-Armour said.

Simmons' frown deepened. "What do you pay?" he demanded.

I matched Simmons frown for frown. I didn't like his having spied on us, and I didn't like being asked too many questions.

"Isn't that more or less . . . our business?" I said.

Simmons' white eyebrows shot up and the corners of his mouth bent down. He shrugged, made another trip around the hat sweatband with his finger, and put his hat back on.

"Well, I hope to God you ain't payin' much," he said. "It's a poor house. Won't be standin' long. Needs a heap of work. Well, guess I better be gettin' on."

He turned and started down our drive toward the road.

"How about your rabbit?" I called after him. "Aren't you going to keep looking?"

Without stopping or turning around, Simmons waved a gnarled hand in the air.

"Naw, he don't amount to much, that one," he shouted back. "He's better off lost!"

On a rainy Monday morning two days after we had unloaded, I drove the truck into San Francisco to see what the dealers would offer for it. Without its three-ton load of furniture and knickknacks, the truck accelerated like a sports car. I whistled all the way into town, thinking of the killing we would make when we finally got it sold.

The reaction of the first used-truck dealer I called on was not especially encouraging.

"How much you gotta get outa this heap?" he asked.

When I told him, he snorted and walked back into his office.

I tried half a dozen other dealers after that. Only two of them hung around long enough actually to make an offer. And both offers, I felt, were ridiculously low.

The obvious answer was to sell the truck privately. That night Mary-Armour and I co-authored an advertisement and phoned it to a San Francisco newspaper. There wasn't much time to be lost—we knew that Og would have our hundred machines on location before long, and we were counting on the sale of the truck to provide the $2,656 we still had to fork over.

The following Saturday, Sven came along. Sven was a breezy young Swede with crew-cut blond hair and honest blue eyes. He wore balloon-spinnaker slacks of faded denim, and a bright yellow sport shirt that featured monkeys climbing tall brown coconut trees.

We loved Sven immediately, because Sven loved our truck. Or maybe we loved him because the price didn't give him a coronary. He even said—out loud, too—that it seemed quite fair.

It wasn't long before we discovered why Sven could afford to be so free and easy in money matters. Sven was in the profitable chinchilla-raising business.

"I've only been raising the little rascals three years," he told us, "but last year I reported an income of more than $31,000." An Internal Revenue agent would have licked his lips at the way Sven said "reported."

"Yes," Sven continued, "chinchillas is a nice little business. If you're good at it, you do wonderful. If you're just fair, you do pretty darn good. And even if you're not much of a hand with the little rascals, you still make money."

Sven's somewhat tiresome narration of the joys of chinchilla-raising extended through most of two hours and three beers, but we listened courteously and thoughtfully. After all, Sven was a prospect the like of which we'd never seen.

Finally he came to the point.

"Now what I'd like to do," he said, "is to trade you some chinchillas for the truck."

I leaped out of my chair. "You want to *what?*"

"Trade you chinchillas for the truck," he said. "I'd overtrade you in animals by a good margin—that is, I'd give you a thousand dollars more in animals than you're asking for the truck. What do you say?"

I wanted to say that the No-Name Vending Machine Company, to which we were about to owe $2,656, would probably take a dim view of being paid off in small, furry animals! But instead I merely said something about needing a little fresh air. After Sven had gone, of course, I made a little wax model of him, and Mary-Armour and I took turns sticking pins in it.

Two days later a man who gave his occupation as a "chicken sexer" arrived from Petaluma and endeavored to set us up in the profitable chicken-raising business in exchange for the truck. Two days after that, the owner of a nearby feed store offered to take the truck off our hands and let us take out our asking price in sacks of grain.

I knew, however, that there was only one kind of chicken feed No-Name would accept. So we kept on advertising, meanwhile, of course, trying to figure out our financial strategy, should No-Name finish setting out our route before we got the truck sold.

Whether the truck sold quickly or not, however, one thing was certain: we wanted No-Name to hurry up with the route. Therefore, on January 8, exactly one month after signing the contract, I telephoned San Francisco and got Og on the phone.

"Og," I said, "Jim Nelson."

"Well, hello, Jim!" Og said jovially. "How's everything?"

"That's what I want to ask you," I said. "How's . . ."

"How's the family?"

"They're fine," I said. "When do you think . . ."

"Can you talk a little louder?" Og said. "I don't think we've got a very good connection."

I raised my voice. "When do you think—"

"How's the little one?" Og said. "It's a girl, isn't it?"

"It's a boy," I said. "He's fine."

"Good, good," Og said. "Well, glad you called. Drop in when you're in town and . . ."

"Listen, Og," I said, "when are you going to get those machines on location?"

"What?"

"When are you going to get those machines out?"

"What did you say about a sewing machine? Boy, what a lousy connection!"

"I hear *you* perfectly," I said. I spoke very slowly. "When-are-you-going-to-get-my-machines-out-on-location? It's January 8. I want to get started."

"Oh, your *gum* machines," Og said. "Oh. Well, don't you worry, boy. We're getting them out just as fast as we can."

"How fast is that?" I asked. "I mean, when do you think they'll all be on location?"

"You wouldn't want us to do a rush job and botch it, would you?" Og said. "It takes time, you know, to get the right locations."

"I know," I said. "All I want to know is when can I expect to be in business. I'm not telling you to hurry. I just want to plan ahead a little."

"Well, don't you worry, boy," Og said cheerfully. "Just leave everything to us. Your machines will be out in no time. Drop in and see us when you're in town—okay?"

"Og, I want to know . . ."

"And say hello to the wife. Haven't met her yet—want to, though. And the little girl. Say hello to both of them."

"Og . . ."

I heard a rapid clicking, a few squawking noises, and then the dial tone. I hung up slowly.

Two days later Mary-Armour and I dug into our savings and bought a tired, old, secondhand Jeep station wagon. We'd need something to travel in when the truck was sold, which we hoped would be soon.

On that same day, our first copies of *Billboard* and *Vend* arrived through the mail. Mary-Armour and I began a close study of both, hoping to find a potful of helpful hints for eager young vending-machine operators.

Billboard, a weekly trade paper of the amusement industry, provided a number of interesting—if not very help-ful—facts. Our first discovery was that we could gauge the degree of respectability of any avocation merely by count-ing the number of pages between the front page and the section that dealt with the business in question. The larger the number of pages, the larger the gap between that business and the nice stable occupations that normal people engage in.

You will find news of the radio and television industry, therefore, near the front of the paper. This indicates a relatively high degree of respectability, only slightly above the section that follows, which is devoted to phono-graph records and deejays. (In *Billboard*ese, that's a disk jockey.)

Lay readers of the paper will do well not to proceed beyond this point, however, without adequate supplies of boiled drinking water and a guide, for the course *Bill-board*'s editors have charted is a trek through the lush jungle of state fairs, carnivals, animal trainers at liberty, hippopotamuses for sale, freaks, phonemen ("to work on promotion for Lord's Last Supper"), wagon men, paper men, hanky-pank manufacturers, and purveyors of tattooing supplies.

The editors finally pull up for a breather at an ingenu-ous little column called "Pipes for Pitchmen," in which streetmen—those fellows who stand on street corners sell-ing wind-up toys, vegetable graters, and eyeglass cleaner —exchange homely notes of friendship, and advise one another about the prevailing attitudes of the law enforce-ment agencies in towns they have worked recently.

During this rest period, we might as well go into the problem of "the worker." Surely you've stood on a frosty street corner about the third week in December and heard the beguiling cry:

"Get your giant Santa Claus balloon right here. Only a

few left. Take a beautiful, life-size Santa Claus balloon—painted in three different colors—home to the kiddies tonight!"

"How much?" you ask.

"Only twenty-five cents," the pitchman replies.

You look at the seven-foot-high gas-filled balloon floating dreamily above the pitchman's head, tethered to a string in his left hand. You know that a quarter is a lot of money for one balloon. But so what—isn't it nearly Christmas? And, after all, isn't that the biggest goddam balloon you've ever seen? The kids will be crazy about it!

"I'll take one," you say. You hand over your quarter and receive in return a small piece of colored rubber. You get home. "I bought you kids a Santa Claus balloon," you say.

The offspring are delighted.

"A balloon, a balloon!" they say. "Blow it up, Daddy!"

In getting the balloon started, you nearly burst a lung; it seems that somehow the balloon you bought won't inflate. But then, as you huff and puff for the tenth time and your face turns purple, it suddenly accepts air and begins to expand. The children shriek with joy. You're a real hero!

"What a lovely balloon—it's Santa Claus!"

"Wait till you see—" you pant, gasping for breath—"how big it gets!"

The balloon is now about a foot long. You empty your lungs into it once more. It's a foot and a quarter long now, but something's funny—you'd swear that was about as big as you could blow it. But then you think of the huge balloon on the street corner, the seven-foot-long number. You inhale. You put your lips to the balloon. You blow.

Bang!

Now you know the difference between your balloon and a "worker" balloon. In *Billboard,* workers are advertised at fifty cents apiece, while the ordinary balloon the pitchman sells you—same Santa Claus pattern, of course—can be had for five bucks a gross.

But hop back on your feet, men—the *Billboard* white hunter is signaling us to fall in single file behind him to continue our trip through his periodical. Now he is sucking in his breath, shutting his eyes, and plunging headlong into the vending-machine swamp. For several pages we wade through bulk venders up to our chests, while a crocodile named Dentyne snaps his ragged jaws, and Cinnamon Chiclet snakes slither past our knees. Before we emerge on the other side, one or two bearers have disappeared with anguished cries beneath the murky surface.

Our safari finally ends (after an innocuous side trip into nickelodeons) with a glamorously wicked section on pinballs, shuffle games, and slot machines. We are now, of course, a long way from the front page and the kind of business you bring home to Mother.

Mary-Armour and I loved poring over *Billboard*, but it was in *Vend* that we read something that staggered us. *Vend* is a monthly magazine put out by the same people who publish *Billboard*, and is, as the name suggests, devoted exclusively to the vending field. In *Billboard*, the vending-machine man is in with the bums. In *Vend*, he is king.

"How come we got two copies of *Vend* this month?" Mary-Armour asked me one morning. We were sitting out on our wonderful lawn, reading the day's mail and lapping up the wonderful dappled sunshine that filtered through our 400-year-old oak trees.

"The one you're reading is the regular monthly issue," I said. "The one I've got is the *Vend Almanac*."

"What's the *Vend Almanac?*"

"Oh, it gives a lot of dope, like where you can buy machines, and how much they cost, and stuff like that."

"Oh."

"Looks very comprehensive," I said.

"Does it list the kind of machines we're buying?" Mary-Armour asked.

"I guess so," I said.

"Look and see."

I flipped through the pages of the *Almanac*. "Let's see, here it is—no, those are cigarette machines—yes, here it is. It says . . . *My God!*"

"What?"

"Why, those dirty crooks! Those sons of—"

"What's the matter, sweetie?"

"We're being robbed!" I said. "We're paying $52 a copy for our machines, and do you know how much they list for here?"

"How much?"

"They run $17.35 for the bulk vender, and $22.95 for the tab-gums!" I sprang out of my chair and hurled the *Vend Almanac* to the ground. "Those robbers! I'll kill 'em!" I said. I strode purposefully toward the Jeep, which was parked in front of the house.

"Where are you going?" Mary-Armour asked.

"I'm going to San Francisco," I said, "and I'm going to get Og Chugwater by his fat, pink neck, and I'm going to crack his skull against the first $52 vending machine I can lay my hands on!"

"You can't go in your bathing trunks," Mary-Armour said.

I looked down. "Oh," I said. I sprinted into the house and started dressing. Mary-Armour followed me into the house, carrying Jamie in her arms.

"Sweetie," she said, as I stared grimly into the bureau mirror, knotting my necktie, "be careful. Please?"

"Chugwater's the one that better be careful," I said.

"Don't get in a fight," she said.

"I can't promise a thing," I said.

I slipped my wallet into my back pocket, picked up the car keys, and started for the front door. Mary-Armour followed me out to the Jeep.

"Just be careful, darling," she said. "Don't do anything foolish. Remember you haven't been in a fight since fifth grade."

"Yeah?" I said gruffly. "Who told you that?"

"You," she said. "Listen, darling, I'm on *your* side. Did you know that?"

I turned and looked at her, standing there with her pretty blue eyes opened wide, and Jamie in her arms, unconcerned, playing with her beads.

"I'm sorry," I said. "I don't know why I should be taking it out on you." I kissed her and climbed into the Jeep. "Don't worry."

I felt momentarily chastened that I had been so abrupt with Mary-Armour, but by the time I reached No-Name's neighborhood, my rage was back at fever heat. The paper-thin tires on the little Jeep smoked ominously as I skidded to a stop in front of the No-Name office, thrust a nickel into the parking meter, and burst into the building.

Truss and Og were sitting side by side at a table near the front of the display area. Og stood up, a cherubic smile enveloping his smooth, round face, and extended a fat be-ringed hand.

"Jim, boy!" he said jovially.

I ignored the outstretched hand.

"Listen, you birds!" I snarled. I let the lid blow right off. "What are you trying to do—bilk me?"

Og's eyebrows shot up so far I thought they were going to join his frowzy crew cut. Truss's eyebrows, on the other hand, undulated up and down in a sort of wave motion, as though they couldn't decide just what emotion to portray. Both men were speechless as I told them, using the colorful idiom of the U. S. Navy, exactly what I had discovered in the *Vend Almanac,* and how I felt about it. I wound up my tirade with the words, "What the hell kind of a blank-blanking deal is this, anyway?"

Truss recovered the power of speech first. His eyebrows had settled down and were portraying surprise, tinged with sorrow.

"Why, Jim, boy," he said, pouring an experimental barrel of oil onto the troubled waters, "I don't think you appreciate the difficulty of getting these machines on location. First, those prices in *Vend* are a little low. You see, actually, the machines cost us a couple of dollars more because of freight from the factory. And then, you've got to realize that they come to us *raw,* unadjusted."

"We have to adjust them," Og said, straightening his spotted necktie. "Every last one of them has to be adjusted."

"Naturally, they have to be loaded with merchandise, too," Truss continued, "and the merchandise costs money."

Og shot his cuffs and nodded affirmatively.

"It ain't free, brother!" he said.

"And then, most of your machines will be placed on stands, Jim," Truss said, "and stands cost money, too."

"Stands are damn expensive," Og interjected, "and that's the truth!"

Now it was I who proved speechless. I felt hot, I felt outraged, and yet I had to admit that stands did cost money, and so did merchandise.

Truss pinched the bridge of his skinny nose delicately with an embalmed thumb and forefinger.

"Then you've got the cost of locating the machines," he said. "That's certainly not a cheap operation. We have to send out specialists out onto the road to find the best locations in your territory. And believe me, they get paid plenty to do the job right, because if they pick a bad location, they lose their locating fee. You can't scrimp on getting locations."

"No, sir!" Og seconded.

Truss smiled at me and turned his palms outward. His waxy face displayed the smile of a patient saint, an understanding father, a Christian martyr forgiving the lion for nibbling at his heels.

"You don't think we're getting rich doing this kind of work, do you?" he asked, simply. "We're not. We make a very small margin of profit."

There were no two ways about it—I was lost.

My God, the reader screams! Are you going to let them get away with that? What kind of fool would let a couple of highbinders—highbinders on whom he actually has the goods—get away with that kind of swindle?

I have asked myself the same question many a time since. All my journalistic training had taught me not to believe anyone unless he could prove every word he said. As a magazine editor I constantly doubted the pronouncements of men high up in big corporations, and yet here I was, wandering along, idly picking daisies and believing 89 per cent of the sea stories handed out by those old yarn spinners, Ogden Chugwater and Truslow Thomas.

All I can say is that I was hypnotized. Somehow I knew that the wool was being pulled down over my eyes, ears, and navel, but I kept seeing that Unholy Grail before me —a hundred dollars a week for two days' work. Provided, of course, that No-Name finally unlimbered and got its men of science out on the road, scratching up a few locations.

Put yourself in my position. See what you'd do. You've moved into a house of your own, and have rent to pay. You want to get your carefully planned Good Life into actual operation. You have food to buy, a truck to sell. Your savings account has a leak in it. You've got the prospect of

57

a hundred dollars a week to sustain you as soon as your machines get out on location. Get that, Buster—*a cool hundred a week for two lousy days' work!* Don't you think you could forgive No-Name if they tried to pick up a few extra bucks in the course of putting you on Easy Street?

I stayed clear of No-Name for a couple of weeks after that. Og had promised to call me very soon—when he was ready to turn some machines over to me. Each day I expected his call. Each day, of course, it didn't come. Each day I felt my old anger return, just a little more than the day preceding.

Finally, when the last week in January arrived, and Og still hadn't phoned, I decided the time had come for the big showdown. I would go to San Francisco, and I would force No-Name to put my machines on location immediately, or give me my money back!

My jaw was set, my eyes were steely as I walked into No-Name once more. I was ready to do battle. This time, the blood in my eye was cold blood.

Truss spotted me the instant I set foot inside the door.

"Well, well, Jim Nelson!" he said, with all the cordiality he could muster. His eyebrows fluttered up and down over his sad eyes like little birds. "Welcome, Jim Nelson. Og was just about to call you, weren't you, Og?"

"Beg pardon?" Og said. "Oh . . . yes! Yes, I was just about to call you, Jim, old boy!"

"Og is ready to start turning machines over to you," Truss said. "Aren't you, Og."

"That's right," Og said. "Rightee-oh, we're all set. Yes, sir. What's a good day for you to meet me in Petaluma, Jim?"

"How about tomorrow?" I said.

"Dandy, dandy," Og said. He leaned forward and riffled his calendar with his jeweled left hand. "Oops! I'm busy tomorrow. Now isn't that a darn shame. Tell you what—how about, uh, two weeks from next Friday? That's February eleventh. Okay?"

Frankly, it wasn't okay. It was just too doggone far in the future. I was about to blow my stack and say so when I heard the old voodoo music again. *Whoo-ee-oo, if any simple rube can make $100 a week out of 100 machines, a cagey, educated business type like yourself can make $125. Maybe $150! Whoo-ee-oo, Truss and Og are your friends, your friends, your friends* . . .

On the morning of February eleventh at a quarter to ten—I was wearing Mary-Armour's wrist watch instead of my own; I didn't want to take any chance of being late—I pulled the Jeep to a halt in front of the Petaluma post office, where Og had said he would meet me at ten. I searched the street for the salmon-colored Crosley station wagon Og said he would be driving. I knew I was early, so I bought a copy of the San Francisco *Examiner* and began to read the vending-machine ads. I scoffed at the juicy blue-sky copy that I now knew by heart. "Invest $500, make $50 a week," indeed! Ought to be in jail!

Every two minutes I cased the street for the walking jewelry store. Finally at five minutes after ten I realized that Og must be waiting *inside* the post office. Probably he had got there before me and was wondering where *I* was.

I got out of my car and went in. No Og. I went back to my car and read the rest of the Business Opportunities ads. "Gas station. Pumps plenty. 100% location. Sacrifice due to illness." Why, I asked myself, would anyone get into a tiresome, time-consuming business like running a filling station when there were lucrative deals available, like vending?

By 11:30 I had read every word in the *Examiner*, worked the crossword puzzle, and checked the inside of the post office four more times. I began to read the notice tacked on the post-office wall, telling the time and date of the next civil service examination. My eyes wandered on past a recruiting sign for the Marine Corps and stopped on a "Wanted" sign. I felt a chill all the way to the marrow as I read:

> WANTED for mail fraud and probation violation. Howard Lee Goodfellow, alias John H. Gooding, John Howard Gooding, Howard Lee Truehart, Jerry.
>
> Description: White; born Keokuk, Iowa, December 13, 1912; height 6' ½"; weight 195 lbs.; blond wavy hair, good dresser, convincing talker.
>
> Offenses: Under the alias of John H. Gooding, and as Vice-President of Trueheart Vending Corp., Minneapolis, Minn., Goodfellow engaged in selling franchises for the distribution of vending machines by means of false and fraudulent pretenses, representations, and promises. He was placed on probation for 3 years at Birmingham, Ala., on June 23, for use of the mails in operation of the scheme. However, he resumed his fraudulent operations in St. Louis, Mo., and Atlanta, Ga., and his probation, therefore, was revoked. He was indicted at Atlanta, Ga., on October 2. He disappeared from Atlanta on November 18, accompanied by his wife, Jane Vera Traxlar (maiden name) who is a beautician. The U. S. Marshals at Atlanta, Ga., and Birmingham, Ala., hold warrants for the arrest of this subject under the name of John H. Gooding. If located please cause his immediate arrest and notify the undersigned or nearest Post Office Inspector by telephone, telegraph, or teletype, collect.

A. E. Helmick	M. H. Ackerman
P. O. Inspector in Charge	P. O. Inspector in Charge
Chattanooga 1, Tennessee	Atlanta 2, Georgia

With sickening suddenness I realized what had happened. I hadn't seen Truss and Og for two weeks. That had given them a wealth of time to make their getaway.

Chances were they'd brought a lot of other suckers to the boiling point at the same time they had me, and the two of them were probably lolling on some beach in Mexico right that minute! It was small comfort to realize that at least they hadn't got the second $2,600, even if they had conned me out of the first.

I was heading for a telephone booth to relay my lugubrious news to Mary-Armour when I stumbled over Og. Genial, bloated, smiling Og.

"Oh, there you are," he said, tipping his head back and peering at me through the bottom of his bifocals. "I've been looking all over for you."

"Where've you been looking?" I demanded.

"All up and down the street," he said. "I had no idea you'd go inside, but when you didn't show up, I figured I'd better have a look."

"When *I* didn't show up!" I said. "How long have you been here?"

"Over an hour," he said. "But never mind. It's okay. Let's get started, though, now that you're here."

I was seething, but I was also greatly relieved to find that Og was not in Acapulco. His picture didn't belong on the post-office wall after all—at least not yet. And since I couldn't see where getting mad would get me, I got calm instead. Besides, I told myself, as soon as I got my hundred machines, I could spit in Og's left eye if I felt like it!

Og pulled a bunch of white cards from his pocket and began to shuffle through them. "Let's see," he said, "we'll start by going to the Doodle Diner. You've got one machine there. You know where Third Street is?"

We found Third Street, and we found the Doodle Diner, a tiny, elongated restaurant covered with neon beer signs, and placards reading "Truckers Welcome!" Inside, at one end of the counter sat—I felt my heart leap as I saw it—My Machine!

The machine was already covered with a generous coating of grease, as was everything in the Doodle Diner, including the customers. I pulled out my handkerchief and wiped the machine off. The route card, which bore the name of the location, address, key number, and commission (20 per cent in this case) listed the proprietor of the Doodle Diner simply as "Sis." I wasn't sure how to proceed, but Og Chugwater, man of the world, soldier of gumball fortune, knew what to do. Boldly he addressed a skinny middle-aged woman with an incredibly frizzy permanent, who was standing behind the counter.

"Hello, Sis," he said. "We're just checking the machine. This is Jim—he owns the machine, and he'll give you good service."

Sis's voice came right out of her nose.

"I think it's dewin' right well," Sis said. "Don't yew?"

"It's doing fine," Og agreed heartily. "And it's a fine machine, Sis. These machines cost more than fifty dollars apiece. Did you know that?"

"Dew tell!" Sis said.

"Jim here'll keep an eye on it," Og said, as we started to leave.

"That's right," I said, tipping my hat—"Sis."

Frankly, the Doodle Diner fell somewhat below the quality of location I had expected, but I felt I mustn't be hasty in judging. For one thing, I realized that this was merely the first location, and that we still had ninety-nine machines to go. Besides, I felt that if No-Name's expert locating staff felt this was a good spot for a machine, it probably was. After all, those boys knew.

The Trip-Trap, another greasy-spoon eatery across the street from the Doodle Diner, was our second port of call. Our third stop was a respectable-looking market presided over by what turned out to be the oldest young man in the world, a dour chap named Emerson Thigpen. On the route card I noted that Thigpen was getting 25 per cent of the gross. This was 5 per cent higher than Og had previously told me I would have to pay. I asked him about it.

"Oh, that," Og said breezily. "Wherever we've had to give 25 per cent, we've set the machine a little finer to make up for it."

"You mean, so it doesn't give out so much for a penny?"

"That's right," Og said. "The kids don't know the difference."

Since these particular machines were vending gumballs, one for a penny, I didn't quite see how you could set them to give each customer a smaller portion. But I let the idea pass, and we left the store. (Some months later, incidentally, when I found out that Sourball Em Thigpen was brother-in-law to the No-Name scientist who had secured the locations, I felt lucky I wasn't paying him 90 per cent!)

Og turned six more machines over to me before he headed back to San Francisco. Two were in a launderette, one in a spot merely called "Café," one in another Doodle-Diner-type restaurant called Pancho's Rancho, and two in a busy-looking grocery store called Cobwell's Market. I now had ten machines in all and was, therefore, one-tenth of the tycoon I would eventually be.

Og gave me some merchandise for refilling the machines, and a bill for the merchandise. He also gave me a scale for weighing the pennies (instead of counting them), some penny wrappers, some receipt books, and a bill for those too. I was in business.

Og promised to call me very soon to turn over some machines in Santa Rosa. He implied that it would be any day now.

But, of course, it wasn't.

5

No mother hen ever looked after her brood more solicitously than I after our tiny flock of machines during those first rainy weeks. Two days after my meeting with Og, I was back in Petaluma, clucking noisily.

Three days passed before I felt the urge to service our machines again—or at least before I gave in to it. I loaded the car with the merchandise Og had given me. Whistling, I went back into the house, sought out Mary-Armour, and kissed her.

"Thought I'd take a little ride," I said. "Want to come along?"

"Where are you going?"

"Oh, I don't know. Petaluma, I guess."

"Why are you going to Petaluma?"

I tried to look innocent. "I just thought I'd have a look

—you know, see how things are going. And it's such a lovely day . . ."

"It is not. It's misting."

"Well, my typewriter's being cleaned down in San Rafael, you know," I said.

"What's that got to do with it?"

"Well, I thought maybe I'd pick it up—and just sort of drive through Petaluma on the way down. It's on the way, you know."

"It is not on the way, and you know it," Mary-Armour said. "You're just going to Petaluma to see if we're rich yet, aren't you?"

I scratched my head. "Well, not exactly. I just thought . . ."

"And you want someone to go along so you won't feel quite so foolish at having been there three times in a week. Right?"

"Well, I don't think of it quite that way," I said, "although I'd welcome the company. Of course, it *is* misting, you know."

"Nonsense," Mary-Armour said. "It's a lovely day. Just a minute till I put some clothes on your son."

We were just ready to turn out of the drive when a short, broad-beamed old troll in overalls and a straw hat stepped out from behind our gate and held up his hand. I stopped the car. Mr. Simmons, the prune raiser, walked up to my window, his small, lively eyes darting around the inside of the car, cataloguing the contents.

"Haven't seen a—" he stood on tiptoe and craned his neck at the boxes of gum behind the back seat—"a little speckled doe-rabbit, have you?"

"I'm sorry, I haven't," I said. "Have you, sweetie?"

Mary-Armour shook her head. "Sorry," she said.

"See you're haulin' a few things," Simmons said, nodding toward the back of the Jeep.

"A few," I said.

"Boxes of stuff, it looks like," he said.

"That's right," I said, "it's just boxes of stuff."

"Says chewing gum on the box," he said.

"Mr. Simmons," I said, "not only is your eyesight twenty-twenty, but I am going to take a load off your mind. I'm going to tell you all there is to know about us."

"Well, I'm not pryin'," Simmons said.

"Of course not," I said. "Nevertheless, I think that since we're neighbors, and since you have already told us about your prune, rabbit and chicken raising, it's only fair for me to tell you that we are in the vending-machine business."

"What's vending machines?"

"You put a penny in one of them," Mary-Armour said, reaching into a box in the back seat and picking up half a dozen sticks of gum, "and out comes this." She reached across me and gave the gum to Simmons. "Here. Try some."

"Well, now, I'll be!" Simmons said, looking at the gum in his hand admiringly. "You mean this here's for me?"

"All yours, Mr. Simmons," Mary-Armour said, smiling.

Simmons scratched his head and wiped his nose on his sleeve. Then he opened three sticks of gum, one after the other, and wadded them into his mouth.

"Well, what do you know!" he said. "I sure didn't guess you were in *this* business. I seen an empty gum carton out by your pumphouse—I was lookin' for one of my rabbits," he added hastily, "they're always runnin' off, you know—but I sure never guessed nothin' like this!"

"Well, that's the story," I said.

Simmons chewed silently for a moment.

"Well, guess I oughta be movin' along," he said. "Got to ride my old motorsickle into town and get 'er fixed." He pursed his lips and looked at me as though he was about to reveal something confidential.

"By the bye, that old house of yours," he said, "I

wouldn't worry too doggone much about 'er. It's been standing for a long time. I guess she ain't ready to give out yet."

We smiled noncommittally, waved, and started down the road toward Petaluma.

Three-quarters of an hour later, while Mary-Armour and Jamie sat outside in the car, I stood inside Thigpen's grocery, squinting at the gum-filled glass globes on the two venders. I couldn't quite make up my mind whether the left-hand machine, which three days ago had been five-eighths full, according to the notation I had made on my route card, was now half full or fifteen-thirty-seconds empty.

"Whatcha doin'?"

I turned around quickly to face dark-browed, iron-jaw Emerson Thigpen himself. Arms folded, he glowered at me like a threatening thundercloud.

"I was just checking the machine," I said.

"You weren't taking any money out, were you?"

"No, I only . . ."

"Don't *ever* take the money out unless I'm here personally," he said.

"No, I won't."

"*See* that you don't!" he said, turning away.

His remarks left me slightly nettled. I felt almost as though he had accused me of stealing. But I chalked it up to the weather and supposed that he had just crawled out from the wrong side of the rock that morning. I finished making my notations and went back to the car.

The machine in the Doodle Diner had a fresh coat of cooking grease, which I removed carefully with my handkerchief. I made a notation in my pocket notebook to bring a cloth with me on future servicing trips.

The last two machines I looked at were the two at Cobwell's Market. I pulled to the curb, turned off the engine, and was starting to get out when I saw something electrifying. There was a little girl, a golden-haired tot of about five years, hovering around our machines, and *she had a penny in her hand!*

"Look," Mary-Armour said, "that girl's going to . . ."

"Shhhhhhhhhhh!" I hissed. I sat stock-still, hardly daring to breathe lest I frighten her away.

The little girl looked at our tab-gum vender, first at the front of it, then the back. Then she looked at the ball-gum vender beside it. A sudden noise down the street distracted her for a moment. Soon, however, probably because of the telepathic waves with which I was swamping her, she returned her attention to the machines. She raised her tiny hand toward the coin slot on the ball-gum machine. The penny caught a reflection, glistened briefly. Then it dropped onto the sidewalk.

"For crying out loud!" I said under my breath to Mary-Armour. "Kids are certainly careless with their money nowadays! You'd think it grew on . . ."

But wait, she'd found the penny again. She was really a pretty child, sweet, demure, dressed all in blue. Once again she reached for the coin slot. This time the penny went in. The little girl turned the handle. A gumball clinked down the escape hatch into the child's hand. A millisecond later she popped the gumball into her mouth.

I jabbed Mary-Armour with my elbow.

"Get that, kid!" I said.

She turned and smiled at me. "It was beautiful, wasn't it."

"Beautiful?" I said. "Is that the best you can do? It was a warm human drama of American capitalism, chock-full of stirring emotional conflicts, but with a smash-up happy ending guaranteed to tug at your heartstrings! That, baby, was *a sale!*"

Our drive back from Petaluma that day was, needless to say, a gloriously happy thing. All was right with the world.

As we passed the tallow factory on the edge of town, we saw the first of many glossy red-winged blackbirds, and a mile or so later we surprised two coveys of quail, skittering across the road like so many dowagers in tiaras. Jamie smiled at the sleek dairy cattle, and Mary-Armour nodded sympathetically at a few sad-looking whiteface steers that looked about ready for the deep freeze.

Driving out of Lakeville, we saw a hawk standing absolutely still in the air, riding what must have been an almost perfect updraft over a small bare hill across a gulch from the road. The road was traveled mostly by farmers in pickup trucks, but this day we saw a Rolls-Royce rolling swiftly toward us, headed for Petaluma. At the time, I wouldn't have been at all surprised to learn that it was a brother vending-machine operator.

One cool morning exactly a week later, I set out—alone this time—with a fresh globe of ball bubble gum to exchange for the partially depleted one in front of Cobwell's Market. Jauntily clad in crisp, clean khaki pants, a sport coat, and a nutmeg-brown J. Press hat, I stepped up to the first machine.

I inserted the key in the lock. I was determined to be good at my job. I was going to get this servicing business down to the point where it took practically no time whatever, thereby giving myself plenty of leisure to Do Interesting Things.

I turned the key briskly. I opened the door of the machine. I pulled a lever. I lifted the globe out. I unscrewed the metal vending mechanism from it. I was Mr. Efficiency. Quickly I carried the depleted globe to the Jeep, exchanged it for a full globe, and began to screw the vending mechanism back on.

But it wouldn't go. I urged it. I twisted it counterclockwise. I tried forcing it. Obviously wrong. I swore. I coaxed. I muttered a few crude pronouncements about Ogden Chugwater's parentage. But it all did no good.

Between struggles, I noticed that the glass globe and the metal vending mechanism each bore a small red mark. Brushing aside the possibility that it was my own blood, I lined up the two red marks and gave the vending mechanism a twist. It went on as beautifully as though Og had done it himself.

I was considerably more cagey as I placed this assembly back into the red metal case. Looking carefully, I found a mark saying "front." I slipped the globe assembly in and smiled as it settled nicely into place. Then I pushed gently on the locking lever, and then harder on the stubborn locking lever, and then I socked the damned-fool locking lever a sharp blow with the heel of my hand, and this time there really was blood!

Fifteen minutes later, bleeding and perspiring, I took a screwdriver out of the Jeep's tool kit and attacked the machine with brute force. After a great deal of grunting, I managed to bend a couple of flanges so that by holding my tongue just right and reciting "Horatius at the Bridge" backward I was finally able to force the locking lever back into position.

If there were any quail, pheasants, Daimlers or Bentleys on the road home that day, I failed to notice them.

During the next month I had four more rendezvous with Og Chugwater—to have him turn more machines over to me—and each time he was late, anywhere from forty-five minutes to two hours and a half. A lesser man might have run out of suitably bizarre excuses for his tardiness. But not Og. His fecundity knew no limit.

"Would have been here sooner, Jim," he told me on the occasion of our second meeting, "but I had an accident on the freeway."

"An accident?" I asked, with more indignation than sympathy. "What happened?"

"I was driving along minding my own business," he

said, hitching up his pants, "in my other car—the new Caddie—and this fellow cut in front of me. Crazy damn fool, zipping along like he owned the highway. I had no choice but to plow right into him!"

"Gee whiz," I said, softening a little. "I hope no one was hurt."

"Both shaken up quite a bit," Og said. He ran a flabby, be-ringed hand across his pink forehead and sighed. It was then that I noticed Og had been forced to take aboard some rather aromatic nerve medicine since the accident, what proof or brand I couldn't tell. "Had to go all the way back to Walnut Creek and put the Caddie in the local garage," Og continued. "Had to come in the station wagon instead."

I didn't believe a word of what Og was telling me—except for the fact he'd come in a Crosley—but I enjoyed the story all the same. I mean, it was well told.

Another time (this was the two-and-a-half-hour wait that set the record) after I had telephoned No-Name from some lonely gumball outpost to inquire where on God's green earth Ogden Chugwater could be, Og himself came on the wire. His diction was rather thick, and he hiccoughed once or twice as he peevishly accused me of having got my dates mixed. Obviously, this was not impossible, although I was so eager to get all the machines under my control that I counted days, hours, and even minutes until the time arrived for another rendezvous with Og.

Whenever Og did finally show up, it was usually lunch time, so that having already lost an hour or so in waiting, I would lose another in eating. Og loved his food. During these lunches, he would finger his gold watch chain and regale me with tales of the $35,000 cabin cruiser he was buying (he was going to have to spend another $10,000 for accessories, however, before it would be exactly what he wanted), of the large staff of salesmen he had once headed in New York, of his incredible ingenuity. He had once repaired an ailing carburetor with a corset stay and a lady's garter—would I believe that? I said I would. And hi-fi—did I think that was something new? Og had made a hi-fi record player back in 1930 out of (as I remember) a Little Giant crystal radio, a windup alarm clock, and an electric heating pad.

In spite of all Og's shortcomings, neither snow nor rain nor heat nor gloom of night could stay him from turning all 100 machines over to me eventually if we just kept meeting often enough. Therefore, on one day so close to the Ides of March that I should have been on my guard, Og and I dropped down out of the high hills on the west side of the Napa Valley into rich vineyard country where, in the towns of St. Helena, Rutherford, and Yountville, I got my ninety-eighth, ninety-ninth, and one-hundredth machines.

"Well, it's all yours, brother," Og said, fumbling for something in his brief case. We were stopped by the side of the road, sitting in the front seat of the Jeep—there wasn't room in Og's Crosley for anything except Og. "Count your cards," he said, "that's one hundred."

I ran a quick tally on my route cards and verified his statement. "I guess you're right, Og," I said.

"Rightee-oh," he said. He pulled a yellow slip of paper out of his brief case. "Ah, here it is. This is the sign-off slip. You sign right here—it shows that I've turned the whole hundred machines over to you."

I read it, signed it, and handed it back.

"And now, if you'll just give me your check for $2,656," he said, "we're all square."

"Right now?" I said.

"Sure," he said. "Why not? You've got the machines, haven't you?"

"Well, yes," I said. I thought of my asset, the truck, sitting over in the Sonoma Valley, unsold. "I'll give you a check in San Francisco, Og," I said.

"Can't you just write it out now?" he said. "I've got several different kinds of blank checks here."

"I can't do it right now, Og," I said. "I'll do it as soon as I can."

"Haven't you got the money?"

"Sure, I've got the money!" I said. "Only it's not in cash. I have to liquidate some of my assets."

"Well, okay," Og said grudgingly. "But try to do it tomorrow, huh?" He pulled a long face. "It's not us so much, Jim," he said, "it's our damn auditors. They pester the life out of us if they see we have an account outstanding."

I promised to try to get No-Name out of the soup with its mean old auditors as soon as I could. Og smiled, held out his boneless hand, and I squeezed it. Before we parted, Og told me that as soon as I had collected some data on how my machines were doing, No-Name would relocate the slow earners for me. Then he reminded me once more about the grim-faced auditors he'd have to face, and we went our separate ways.

Over the dinner dishes that night, Mary-Armour and I debated how to raise the money.

"We could sell the truck right away to a dealer," I said, "but we'd take an awful loss."

"Somehow," Mary-Armour said thoughtfully, "that doesn't seem quite right."

"I agree," I said. "It's a hundred per cent wrong any way you look at it. I'd rather have the auditors burn old Og at the stake than lose money on that truck. But what else can we do?"

"Well, we've got some savings."

"So we're living on the savings," I said. "So we give the savings to No-Name. Then what do we live on?"

"We'll sell the truck eventually," Mary-Armour said.

"Eventually may be a long, long time," I said. "What will we live on in the meantime?"

"Well," Mary-Armour said, "won't we be getting *some* income from the route?"

That struck me as a novel idea. In the long drawn-out negotiations with Og, I'd almost forgot that the route had a purpose.

"I guess we will at that," I said.

"Of course, we *could* just let No-Name wait for a while," Mary-Armour said. "They made us wait two and a half months."

That idea had a certain amount of old-world charm about it, too. But for some unreasonable reason—now unknown and not even to be guessed at—it got lost in the shuffle. Instead, we scraped the bottom of the barrel and came up with a handful of splinters and enough remaining Standard Oil shares to make up $2,656. After a complex and tragically final transaction with Messrs. Merrill Lynch, Pierce, Fenner & Beane, I dutifully handed the money over to Og Chugwater.

Og casually stuffed the check into his top desk drawer and began talking about the big relocating job he was going to do for me some day. He wasn't satisfied—no, sir, not by a long shot—that all my locations were A-Number-One, and he was going to make the locating specialist move some of the machines.

As I walked out No-Name's front door that day, I got a strange, extrasensory sensation that my check was going out the back door, headed toward the bank at a dead run. But what did that matter to me—I had my hundred machines, didn't I?

6

For the next several weeks No-Name and I each went our separate ways. I now had a considerable amount of territory to cover, and I knew that I would have to improve my servicing techniques if I was going to handle everything in two days a week.

I devised two one-day routes, one of which involved about 120 miles of driving, the second about 75. Neither circuit presented much in the way of difficulty, except for the fact that I was new and green and spent a great deal too much time gabbing with store owners and fiddling with the machines.

The sun shone intermittently for about three weeks in a row, and I enjoyed the drives immensely. Mary-Armour and Jamie went with me two or three times, and although stopping to change diapers slowed servicing down a bit, we had fun. There was no doubt about one thing—we had certainly picked a beautiful part of California to live in.

And then it rained for three days, and I didn't care because I was my own boss and could do my servicing any old time I felt like it. I spent the time sitting in our vaulted living room—the previous occupant had been a plastering contractor, and the living-room ceiling rose to a point, like a Persian temple—and read Franz Kafka, because I thought I ought to, and played with Jamie, because I wanted to. By the end of the third day, when the rain stopped, I felt wonderfully rested and had absorbed enough Kafka to get me through most ordinary cocktail parties, which is enough Kafka for anyone. The following morning I set out on my servicing rounds.

Everything was going fine until I got to Freddie Wing Duck's grocery store. The machine was sitting on a portable stand out in front of his store, and although I noticed a few drops of moisture on the outside of the glass globe, it meant nothing to me. I'll just get out my cloth and wipe it off, I told myself. And then Freddie appeared.

Freddie Wing Duck was an incredibly small Chinese-American who stood four feet seven at the outside and couldn't have weighed more than ninety pounds. He was ninety pounds of perpetual motion, however, and if he wasn't heaving hundred-pound sacks of potatoes around as though they were toy bean-bags, he was rearranging the canned goods in some new way or washing the big, spotless front window. As everyone knows, a body in motion tends to stay in motion, and even when Freddie was standing still, talking to a salesman, he would be drumming the counter impatiently with one hand and tapping his foot. Freddie had one blue eye and one brown eye, a "flat-top" haircut—clipped close on top, but long and flowing on the sides—and he was married to the most beautiful Oriental girl I have ever seen. Her name was Moonstone, and she was at least a foot taller than Freddie. Her eyes were wide and very dark; her figure, beneath the high-necked slit-sided Chinese sheath dress she wore, could only be classified as voluptuous. She wore dangling gold earrings that tinkled when she walked, and her long, blue-black hair hung down her back in a single, thick braid tied at the end with a green velvet ribbon. I don't think I ever heard Moonstone speak a word of English. Freddie gave her orders in Chinese, and she hurried to obey. When she had completed the task set for her, she would go and stand at the rear of the store, her big, soft eyes following Freddie around tenderly.

"Hello, Freddie," I said. Freddie stopped in the front door of his store, two oranges in his left hand, one in his right.

"Hello, gum man," Freddie said. He began expertly to juggle the three oranges. "What happened to machine?" he said.

"Say, you're pretty good at that," I said.

Freddie kept on juggling, barely looking at the oranges. "Damn thing stuck," he said.

"The machine?"

"Damn thing no work," he said. "Moonstone try it this morning. Got no gum." Freddie caught the three oranges and began hopping up and down on his right foot. "You fix, eh?"

"Sure, I'll fix it," I said.

"Moonstone lose her penny," Freddie said.

"I'll gladly refund that," I said, digging, into my change pocket.

"No, no, no, no, no," Freddie said. He stopped hopping and juggled two oranges with one hand. "I just tell you, that's all."

"Okay," I said, "I fix."

I inserted the key in the case and opened the door of the machine. A tiny rivulet of colored water poured out and spattered the toe of my shoe.

"Damn thing got water in?" Freddie asked, amazed.

I lifted out the vending mechanism, and a brightly colored, semisolid mass of bubble gum began to ooze gently out of the merchandise slot. It got on my right hand, and when I withdrew my hand, it stretched out in long, sagging sticky strings.

"Freddie," I said, "where've you been keeping this machine during all this rain?"

Freddie stopped juggling and looked up at me innocently. "Right here," he said. "You said this was good spot. Lotta foot traffics."

"There's plenty of foot traffics all right," I said, "but when it rains, the machine has got to come inside the store, Freddie. Otherwise the water gets to the gum and melts the sugar, and . . . this is what happens." I showed him the vending mechanism, completely clogged with the primordial bubble-gum slime. Before I knew it, Freddie had taken the globe out of my hands and was walking back into the store.

"I sure sorry!" he said. "I clean damn thing up."

"It's not your fault, Freddie," I said, starting after him. "Listen, I should have told you the thing wasn't waterproof. Here, give it to me. Cleaning up is my job."

"No, I clean," Freddie said. "I leave it in rain, I clean." He looked toward the back of the store. "Moonstone!"

Moonstone materialized magically in front of him, eyes downcast, smiling slightly.

"Egg foo yung go bragh!" Freddie said. (Or something like that.) He held out the sticky vending globe, which she quickly took from him.

Moonstone said something softly and bowed, as though Freddie had just done her a real favor. Then, with her earrings tinkling musically and her heavy braid swinging behind her, she disappeared into the back storeroom.

"I should be doing that, Freddie," I protested.

"You and I have coffee," Freddie said. He skipped over

to the checkout counter, where a small kettle was boiling away on a hot plate. He brought two thick crockery cups out from below the counter, put a teaspoonful of instant coffee into each, and filled them with water. He handed one cup to me and began to stir his own with quick, nervous strokes.

"I supposed you'd drink tea instead of coffee," I said.

"Agh, tea!" Freddie said scornfully. He reached under the counter again and brought out a half-empty sack of Chinese fortune cookies. I took one, broke it open, and read the fortune out loud.

"The ax may be sharp, but the wise man does not use it on his toenails," I read. Freddie stopped stirring and began to drum the counter with his fingers. "I guess that's a pretty profound thought," I said.

"They written by some Irishman in San Francisco," Freddie said deprecatingly. "But *cookie* pretty good."

By the time we finished our tea, Moonstone was standing in front of Freddie again, holding the globe and vending mechanism, both clean and sparkling. Freddie took it from her and handed it to me. Moonstone, still smiling, and with eyes still averted, withdrew to the shadowy rear of the store.

"Well, gee, thanks, Freddie," I said. Freddie had already started toward the front door; he wanted to see the machine reassembled and working again.

"And thank *you*, Moonstone!" I called. The only answer was a faint tinkling sound.

In the course of the next four hours, I found seven more machines that had sat outdoors for most of three rainy days. And no Moonstones to clean the globes and the magnificently clogged vending mechanisms, either!

I immediately launched a campaign to inform all storekeepers of the great desirability of not letting the machines get wet. I might as well have saved my breath, however, for it became a well-documented fact that not even the most benevolent storekeeper (not even Freddie) could remember to bring a machine in when a downpour started. I'm sure my life insurance company would have canceled my policy, had it known how sadly my life expectancy was shortened each time I saw a gumball machine sitting out in the rain.

Another well-documented fact emerged during the first weeks, and if you ever consider going into the gum-machine business, you may want to know it. It is this: you can set your gum machine down in the most unlikely place—say, the middle of the Sahara—and someone, possibly a camel, will come along and play it. You can lock a machine up in a trunk, weight it with stones, and drop it through a hole in the ice at the North Pole, and when you pull it up, there will be a penny in the coin box. This doesn't mean, however, that the North Pole is a good location, because a second penny may never come along to join the first. It is merely a demonstration of the supernatural nature of gum machines.

The next closest thing to the North Pole as a location was the Trip-Trap Restaurant in Petaluma, where Arna Stanley, the bulky proprietress, could always give me the name and address of anyone who patronized the machine. This job wasn't too hard, actually, since the Trip-Trap never had more than one customer at a time, except during the noon rush, when there might possibly be two.

"My daughter put a penny in last night," Arna told me one rainy Tuesday morning, "and the day before, one of her best girl-friends put in three. I think it's goin' real good, don't you?"

I realized that it wasn't goin' real good, but since I also realized I was probably making as much out of the machine as Arna was out of the whole Trip-Trap, I let it pass.

I left the Trip-Trap, thinking about Og's promise to relocate those machines that weren't up to snuff. Although I knew that it might take a lifetime for Og to get around to the job, I still had some cockeyed kind of faith in the fact that he might eventually do it.

As I drove up the shiny, wet street, I began to wonder if I could afford to wait for Og. Little by little, the thought changed to: *Why* wait for Og? Sure, what the heck, why shouldn't I do a little relocating myself? What Og Chugwater could do, so could Jim Nelson!

I drove out of Petaluma, therefore, and headed for a nearby town where No-Name had seen fit to locate two machines in a moribund hand laundry.

I pulled to the curb on a deserted little side street and walked into the laundry. I found the proprietor, a cauliflower-eared giant, in the back room of his small store, up to his elbows in soapsuds.

"Mr. Hagberry," I said, "I'm afraid I have a rather unpleasant task to perform."

I saw his eyes get big.

"You a process server?" he asked nervously.

"No, no," I said. "I'm the penny-gum man. I'm sorry, Mr. Hagberry, but I'm afraid I'm going to have to take those two machines out."

"Oh, *them*," he said, sighing with obvious relief. "Sure, go ahead, son."

"I really hate to do it, Mr. Hagberry," I said. "I certainly wouldn't, if it weren't for the fact that—"

"Never mind. Take 'em," he said. He flounced a dainty white blouse up and down in the suds.

"Well, it's nothing against your laundry," I said. "It's just that—"

"*Take* the consarned things!" he said, glaring at me.

I stiffened. "Well, if *that's* the way you feel about it—" I said.

"They're just in the doggoned way," Hagberry said. "I was going to have you pick them up this trip anyhow."

I resisted the impulse to dunk Hagberry's head in the soapsuds only because I had an excellent view of his biceps, which were big around as sewer pipes. I marched to the front of his store, divvied up the money (his share was four cents) and lugged the two machines out to the street. There I reloaded them under the shelter of Hagberry's awning, polished them carefully, and put them back in my car. I was now ready for my assault on the juiciest location of them all.

The reason the Gab 'n' Gobble was so juicy was that it stood across the street from a large junior high school. As it was the only store in the vicinity, I figured that it probably did a tremendous business in ice cream, candy, Coke, and other teen-age opiates, and would therefore be a dandy spot to merchandise a few items of my own.

I parked around the corner from the Gab 'n' Gobble, noted that the rain had stopped temporarily, and set my two highly polished machines on the sidewalk—near the store's front door, where they would be easy to get at. Then I walked in. I trembled slightly—it was my maiden voyage.

Lunch hour was just past. Three ladies were mopping up various parts of the store, and a fourth, obviously the Chief, was standing behind the ice-cream cabinet, supervising. She was a big-boned, tough, angular woman, who looked well accustomed to the habit of command. As I approached her, smiling, trying to exude a confidence I somehow didn't feel, she crossed her arms—her muscles rippling.

"Good afternoon," I said. "My name is Jim Nelson, and I live in Sonoma." That was to let her know I was a country man and not a San Francisco slicker. "I operate a small route of gum and candy machines, and I'd like to show them to you."

The lady tipped her head back slightly. Her expression did not change. "Thank you, no," she said. "I've had machines in here, but the kids always break them."

I had the magic solution to that. "We assume all risk of

breakage, madam," I said. "Besides, our machines are extremely durable. I have two out on the sidewalk if you'd care to—"

"Sorry. No machines." Just like that—gentle but firm.

"Maybe we could screw a machine to the counter," I plodded on. "So they couldn't tip it over."

"I'm sorry—no machines." The gentle tone was gone now, and the firmness was increasing rapidly. I was aware of it, but I was so green at the game that I didn't know how to stop.

"Maybe we could—"

"No machines!" she said, her voice starting to rise like a siren. "What's the matter—don't you hear good? How many times do I have to tell you? No machines, no machines, *no bloody machines!*"

"I get it," I said. "Right. Sure. Roger. No machines."

I smiled wanly at the three mopping-up ladies, who were now standing up straight, staring at me, and walked out.

I tried two more small groceries after that—groceries without schools—but it was no dice. The first grocer still carried scars from a brush with some gum operator in Los Angeles, and the other just didn't want to be bothered. Then I tried a chain store.

"Before you could put a machine in here, George," said the manager, a skinny yellow man with a wart on one earlobe, "you'd have to get written permission from the home office."

"And where's the home office?"

"Ramona, Wisconsin, George."

"Could I write them?"

"Can you write?"

I chuckled insincerely over that one. "I wonder if you would be good enough to give me the address, please."

"Two-twenty-two West E Street, George," he said. "Ramona twelve."

"Two-twenty-two—" I wrote—"Ramona twelve. Thank you, sir."

"If they give you the okay," the manager said, "then it's up to me."

"I get the picture," I said. "Okay, I'll write them tonight."

"And since I work on a bonus system where I get a percentage of the net," the manager continued, "and since I sell plenty of chewing gum right over this here counter, and since I get a hell of a sight better markup on it than you'd give me, can you tell me any reason why I should hand that chunk of my bonus over to you?"

I could have shot the dirty double-crosser!

"Sure, I can," I said. "A very good reason!"

"Name it, George," he said.

"I *need* the money worse than you!" I said.

It started to rain again while I was putting my two machines back into the station wagon. I climbed into the driver's seat, and for quite a while I just sat there, staring out at the downpour and thinking up my own corollary to that nothing-succeeds-like-success chestnut—namely, nothing fails like failure. I was one discouraged gumball peddler. I drove around a few blocks, watching the raindrops bounce up off the black pavement, and finally I parked the car in front of a coffee shop and went in for some refreshment.

As the warm, pungent brew seeped into my capillaries, I began to feel faintly revived. I straightened up and looked around. To my surprise, the very coffee shop I was in looked like a fair location for a couple of machines. Not terrific, you understand, but still better than putting them in the hall closet.

Then I heard a miraculous conversation between the proprietor, a ruddy-faced, middle-aged man in a T-shirt and a chef's cap, and one of his customers. Not to have taken advantage of it would clearly have been a sin.

"You forgot your change, Mrs. Argonaut," the proprietor called nasally after a lady who was just leaving. Mrs. Argonaut, sagging with shopping bags and calories, turned from the door.

"Oh, it's just a couple of pennies," she said. She came back nevertheless, and set her bundles down. She picked up the coins and put them in her purse. "You can't get much for a penny nowadays," she said.

"Nope," the proprietor agreed, mopping at the counter with a wet towel. "Used to be a lot of stuff you could get for a penny—newspapers, picture postcards, lots of stuff. Now everything's a nickel."

Bugles blared in my ears, sounding the attack. My feet found the floor. I stood up unsteadily, fighting off an urge to raise my index finger prophetically. The voice I heard croaking from my mouth surely belonged to a stranger.

"I'll tell you something you can still get for a penny," the voice said.

The proprietor and his customer turned toward me.

"One moment, please!" I said. I started for the door. Seconds later, with raindrops streaming down my forehead, I re-entered, panting, lugging two machines and a stand.

"Look!" I said wildly. "For one penny, look what you get!"

The lady customer raised her eyebrows, exchanged looks with the proprietor, and left the store. I smiled toothily at the proprietor. "You see, I happen to operate a string of these," I said, "and I'd be very happy to oblige you by putting one in here. Now, all you have to do . . ."

"Hold it," he said, setting his chef's cap at a rakish angle.

"What's the matter?"

"I know exactly what you're going to say," he said.

"You do?"

"Right. And I believe every word of it. Your machines

look nice, you'll give me good service, your percentage is undoubtedly the highest being offered."

"You took the words right out of my dictionary," I said.

"However, I'm closing this shop," he said. "Moving up the hill. Going to raise camellias."

"Camellias?" I said dumbly.

"Camellias don't chew gum," he said, chuckling and pushing the white cap to the back of his head. "But you probably know that."

I nodded up and down and pressed my lips together. "Okay," I said. "I get the idea. Thanks anyhow." I sort of leaned on one of the machines for a moment and looked out the window. The rain was pelting down by the bucketful.

"Listen," the proprietor said, "really, I wish I could put one of your machines in, but I really *am* going out of business here. That thing I said about camellias chewing gum—I just meant that as a joke."

"Oh, that's okay," I said. Somehow I just didn't have the energy to pick the damn machines up and walk out into the rain.

"Having trouble placing them?"

"A little."

"You ought to try that store up by the junior high," he said. "Lousy with kids. The Gas 'n' Gabble, or something."

"Tried it," I said. "No dice."

The proprietor nodded and scratched a day's growth of beard. "How about some more coffee?"

"Thanks, I'd better get going," I said.

"Oh, come on—on the house. I'll have one, too."

I sat down, and the proprietor filled my cup.

"How about that big market on the west side of town?" he said. "The New China. You tried that?"

"Never even heard of it," I said.

"Listen," he said, "you go out Jackson . . ."

Twenty minutes later, refreshed slightly by coffee and kind words, I stood side by side with Mr. Ying. All the time I was talking to him, he stared impassively out the rain-streaked front window at the cars going by. I ran through my pitch, but I didn't have much enthusiasm left. I knew it sounded hollow. Mr. Ying didn't frown, but neither did he smile. He didn't ask a single question. I knew the next move by heart now—lugging the machines back out into the rain, wrestling them into the Jeep. Slowly Mr. Ying focused his opaque gaze on me.

"You finished?" he said.

I nodded up and down slowly. "Yes, sir," I said. "I'm finished."

"Okay," he said. "Put 'em in."

I almost fell into a large display of Wheaties.

Three days later I pulled two other machines out of a cardroom in Napa. I don't know why I did it. In the first place I had no intention of relocating them myself— I was merely going to turn them over to Og's skilled technicians. And in the second place, this was the only location I had where I could be confident of finding a poker game in progress, no matter what time of night or day I called. Why I considered this an advantage, I'm not really sure now, but I guess I liked the color of the place. There was a counter at the front of the store where the proprietor ostensibly sold cigarettes, and there were four card tables in the back room, along with two of my gum machines. The characters present in this stage setting were all serious career poker players, not one of whom looked to me like the bubble-gum type.

Since the proprietor himself was generally a player in the game, it made it a trifle difficult for me to confer with him on the ailing condition of the two machines. On my first couple of calls I had tried to convince him—between deals—that the machines would do better out on the busy sidewalk in front of his store rather than in the back room with a handful of card players. He disagreed, briefly and with finality.

Maybe that was it—maybe I felt he'd forced my hand. Anyhow, one Friday afternoon, while the sporting men were deep in straights and flushes, I walked in boldly and picked up my machines.

"I'm taking them out," I said gruffly.

The proprietor stared at me wordlessly from beneath his green eyeshade, looking like a poorly made copy of George Raft. I turned my back toward him, lugging the machines out the door, half expecting to be cut down by gunfire, but nothing happened.

The next day I drove to San Francisco and inquired about the relocating work that Og had promised. I was agreeably surprised to have him sit down with me and make out a list of the machines he would have his boys relocate.

"We'll hop on this job right away," Og told me. "Take us about two weeks. Okay?"

I figured that this meant somewhere between four weeks and three months, but anything was better than my having to do the job myself.

"Two weeks would be just fine, Og," I said. "You sure you can do it in two weeks?"

I knew what he'd say next, and he didn't disappoint me.

"Don't you worry one minute, Jim," he said. *"We'll* get the job done!"

7

At last the rains slacked off a little, and the sun began to make its presence felt. I continued to cruise the countryside two or three days a week, servicing machines and waiting for Og to carry out the promised relocating. This interim period gave me a chance to collect a little experience, to start construction of an elaborate aluminum mobile, and to ruminate on the philosophical aspects of the vending-machine way of life.

One thing, at least, was certain: I was now, in my modest way—a way so modest as to be almost pathetic— a tycoon. And so was Mary-Armour, for while I had preempted the title of President of the Multivend Company, she had dubbed herself Chairman of the Board. As a measure of my own tycoonhood, I offer the fact that some of our new California friends rose and saluted as I entered the room at a party one night. I considered this a show of respect befitting my exalted rank, although I could easily have dispensed with their accompanying cry, "Attention, men! Make way for Captain Gumball!"

At a party in San Francisco a week later we found ourselves thrust into the midst of a dinner-jacketed, evening-gowned group, of whom we knew no one but our host and hostess. The usual introductions were made, and then our hostess, in an admirable attempt to get the conversational ball off the ground, said:

"The Nelsons are from Sonoma."

Mary-Armour and I both smiled foolishly, which is about as much as we could do with that kind of remark, and one of the half-circle of ladies facing us said, "Oh, is that so?" which didn't advance the conversation very much, either. I was about to offer something forced about how nice it was for us to get into the city when an expensively groomed blonde in a strapless dress with an extraordinary cantilever effect smiled politely and inquired if we knew Roger and Helen Blackstrap.

"I don't think we've met them," I said. "Do they live in Sonoma?"

"Well, only in the summer, of course," the blonde said. She smiled and let that one sink in, and then she added, "They have a ranch just this side of Glen Ellen. About three thousand acres. Of course, they don't raise anything— it's just a place to relax."

"Sounds adequate," I said.

"Roger bought it about two years ago," the blonde said. She turned to a svelte brunette who was pursuing an olive around the bottom of her cocktail glass with a toothpick. "Remember, Jane," she said, "that was the year Tony and Roger were made vice-presidents." She looked back at us. "Tony's my husband," she confided. "They both made veepee at the same time."

"Well, that was nice, wasn't it," I said. "And what are they veepees of?"

The blonde looked at me, her gently lifted eyebrows echoing the surprise and disbelief in her eyes.

"Why . . . The Bank," she said.

"Oh," I said, nodding up and down. "Sure. The Bank."

Mary-Armour turned to the brunette. "Is your husband in The Bank, too?" she asked.

The brunette stabbed the olive at last and popped it into her mouth.

"God, no!" she said. "All we do is borrow their money. We own a bunch of fruit-processing plants down in the valley. That is, Tom's father does, but he isn't active in the business any more, so I always say 'we.' "

"Well, of course," Mary-Amour said. "It seems like the only natural thing to say."

"And what do you do, Mr. Nelson?" the blonde said.

I felt my pulse quicken alarmingly. There was a certain challenge in the way she said it. I took a quick pull at my martini.

"Well . . . I head up a little retailing chain," I said. "Up north."

I felt Mary-Armour's foot on my toe.

"It's a family deal," I said. "We have about a hundred outlets."

I could feel Mary-Armour's eyes singeing the side of my face.

"Last time I counted it was a hundred, anyway," I said.

This was too much for Mary-Armour's New England conscience. She turned to the two women, dead serious.

"He runs a penny-gum route," she said.

The two ladies and I laughed musically and smiled at one another. It was obvious that no one would believe a cock-and-bull story like that!

Among the people who knew us better, opinion as to our business was split cleanly down the middle. About half our friends considered us overripe for the laughing academy. The other half regarded us in much the same light as Harry Lightfoot, an old college friend with whom I had lunch at Fisherman's Wharf one day when I was in San Francisco picking up merchandise.

"You know, I really envy you, Jim," he said. He turned and looked out the restaurant's big picture window. Beneath us lay a fleet of gaily colored fishing boats; out further was Alcatraz, and off to the left, rising out of a light mist, the Golden Gate Bridge. Harry shook his head, a little misty-eyed.

"You're independent, that's the main thing," he said. "And then, on top of it, you're *coining* dough. I wish I had the guts to make the break."

"We're not really coining dough, Harry," I said. "Actually . . ."

Harry brushed my explanation aside with a wave of his hand.

"I'm not asking for details," he said.

"I know," I said, "but all the same, I think I ought to tell—"

"Security and independence," Harry interrupted, shaking his head slowly. "Boy, I envy you!"

I decided I might as well let him.

The only person who managed to bridge the gap between pity for our addled condition and admiration for our independence was an aged family friend who lived in the Midwest. This dear old soul somehow cherished the misguided thought that Mary-Armour and I were independently wealthy.

"I'm so glad to hear that you have bought the slot machines," she wrote us, "because I am old-fashioned enough to believe that young people of independent means should have a hobby, and not fritter their time away doing nothing."

Well, if it was a hobby, it was a damned expensive one! Our whole financial situation, in fact, was deteriorating rapidly. For one thing, we still owned a large, constantly depreciating truck. And since our income from the route was nowhere near the $100-a-week figure No-Name had blinked at us in colored lights (in fact, it was considerably less than half that), and since our savings account was in the last stages of atrophy, the problem of selling the truck began to emerge as a problem of survival.

We kept our truck ads running in the Sunday newspapers (another drain on our meager resources), and although we got two more queries from the chinchilla set, we still didn't run into anyone with cash in hand. We were urged by various prospects to trade the truck for pasture rental; for a second mortgage on a decaying home the size of an outhouse; for a horse-trailer, complete with horse. Even Simmons, our neighbor, offered a deal. If we would accept his aged "motorsickle" as a down payment (Simmons, we learned, had never owned a car —a bachelor didn't need one, he said), we could take the balance in prunes and poultry, as we needed it. But no one wanted to soil our hands with lucre.

I was busily repairing a broken gum machine one sunny Thursday morning when the phone rang. A gruff voice calling from San Francisco inquired if I was the party with the truck for sale.

"Yes, sir!" I said.

"That thing gotta Brownie?" the voice asked.

Until then, I'd thought a Brownie was some kind of Girl Scout.

"Well, to be perfectly frank," I said, "I'll have to take a look-see. I'll call you back. Okay?"

"Lissen, Buster," the voice said, "if it haddit, you'd know it!"

A Brownie, I found out later, was some kind of fancy gearshift.

With every prospect, it was the same story. Our nice 2½-ton truck, lovely as it was, didn't fit anyone's specifications exactly. Even the chinchilla men claimed they were going to have to alter it extensively. Our prospects gazed at the truck through half-shut eyes, mentally adding a second rear axle, lowering the body, putting in wheelhouses, cutting a side door, inserting a fancier transmission, replacing our 7.50 x 20 tires with larger ones, repainting, insulating, refrigerating. But no one wanted it just as it stood.

Finally we decided to pinpoint our campaign. The heck with newspapers and their waste circulation! We bought a post-card-size mimeograph machine for about fifteen dollars and cranked out five hundred postcards, extolling the virtues of the truck. Then we sat down with the telephone books for San Francisco, Oakland, and half a dozen nearby counties. Every moving, hauling, draying, and transfer company listed in the yellow pages got a card.

This splashy campaign drew four replies. The first three, it turned out, were just window-shopping.

By the time the fourth man invited me to bring the Van Ordinaire to San Francisco for his inspection, we were really beginning to feel desperate. Would it become necessary, we wondered, to move out of our house and commence living in the back of the truck?

Our new prospect, however, was a man of action. While I stood knee-deep in his office carpet, he ordered his shop foreman to take a look at our vehicle. At the same time he telephoned a nearby truck dealer to find out what a similar truck would cost him, new. When the foreman returned and gave our truck a clean bill of health, the big boss took out a yellow pad, figured a year's depreciation, subtracted this figure from the new-truck price, and offered me the balance. It wasn't quite what I'd hoped to get, but on the other hand, it was real, honest-to-God United States money—no chinchillas, no guinea pigs or draft horses, no 1932 Ford pickup to take in trade.

I handed over the title, and he handed over a check, made out in the nicest, biggest, roundest figures I'd seen in a long, long time.

I felt like crying as I bade farewell to the faithful truck that had brought us safely to our new life in California. But there was no time for sentiment in the busy life of a gumball tycoon. I hurried over to No-Name to order some merchandise before hopping a bus back to Sonoma.

Two nights later, Mary-Armour happened to run across the invoice No-Name had made out for the merchandise.

"You ordered seventy boxes of tab gum?" she asked.

I thought a moment. "Seventy? Yes, that's right. Seventy."

"At fifty cents a box?"

"Listen," I said, "you're looking right at the invoice. It *says* fifty cents a box, doesn't it?"

"Yes. I was just asking."

"What's crawling around in your creepy little mind?" I said.

"How many sticks of gum in a box?"

"A hundred. Why?"

"Fifty cents a hundred sticks," Mary-Armour said. "You know, I bet if we can get gum for fifty cents a hundred from No-Name, we can probably get it somewhere else for forty-five."

"Hmm. It's an idea," I said.

"Maybe even for *forty* cents a box," she said. "Get that copy of *Vend,* and we'll write to a few manufacturers."

We shot off an even half-dozen letters the next day, asking various manufacturers if they would be willing to sell us on a direct basis, without the bother—and expense—of going through a middleman like No-Name.

One benevolent chewing-gum company wrote back and said yes, we could buy direct, at forty-five cents a hundred sticks, if we bought certain minimum amounts. This set us up considerably. A second company gave us the same opportunity, except that the minimum quantities they specified were too large for us; the gum would have gone stale—and we would have turned seventy-five—before we could have used it all up. A third outfit, bubble-gum makers, sent back a form letter and a questionnaire, with directions to fill it out and rush it back airmail; on receipt of this information, which would be held confidential, of course, they would let us know their decision.

I filled out the questionnaire immediately and mailed it, eager to hear what our fate would be. The company, however, remained silent (undoubtedly stunned by our replies to their questionnaire). After the first month, I began bombarding them with correspondence, inquiring —politely at first, and querulously at last—when they were going to answer my letter. Finally, a bit of prose directed to the president of the company (a friendly president-to-president kind of letter) elicited a form-letter reply stating that they would sell me direct on such-and-such a basis. When I figured it out, this was exactly the same price I paid No-Name.

A fourth manufacturer who was, as we say in the trade, a big name in Boston Beans (see page 101), never answered at all. Instead, the company merely turned my letter over to No-Name, a corporate indecency from which I have never recovered.

Og chided me about the letter the next time I was in No-Name's office.

"We've been getting some of your letters, Jim," he told me, implying that he had lots of them stashed away in his mysterious desk drawers, "and I want you to know that you can buy merchandise just as cheap here at No-Name as any place in the country—*and some of it cheaper!*

I saw no reason to make any oral disagreement, since Og and I both knew that what he said was not true.

The merchandise itself was pretty colorful, and it was quite a while before Mary-Armour and I got thoroughly sick of sampling it. We handled eight different kinds of tab gum, any one of which you could select from our tab-gum machines for one penny. The economics of the situation worked out like this: one hundred pieces of tab gum cost us about forty-five cents, and, sold through a machine at a penny apiece, brought back one dollar; the grocer or whoever housed the machine got fifteen cents of the fifty-five-cent gross profit, and the remaining forty cents was ours, all ours.

It was all ours, that is, after we paid for gasoline, auto upkeep, auto depreciation, depreciation of the machines themselves, a 3-per-cent bite for the State of California (3 per cent of the gross dollar, not the net), license fees (different in every town), and a bunch of blankety-blank property taxes. A tycoon is not a tycoon unless he damns taxes.

Tab gum was okay in its way, but frankly, right from the start, I was a bulk-vender man. This was not only because the profits were better than on the tab-gum machines, but also because I felt that with enough shrewd thinking on my part, I could make a machine do two or three times the business it had done the previous week. The secret, of course, was to find the right kind of merchandise for each location, and for each time of year. Fortunately, the bulk venders were fairly versatile, and I could switch a bubble-gum machine to selling Boston Beans merely by putting on a fresh glass globe and adjusting the slot that gauged how much each customer got.

The Multivend Company's experience in the case of the Frog Hollow Delicatessen may show you what I mean. The Frog Hollow Delicatessen was operated by Joe Lopez y Garcia, a dark, gloomy, mustachioed native of Los Angeles, who wore a double-breasted pinstripe suit over his sport shirt, and woven, open-toed *huaraches* on his feet. Joe claimed rather proudly to be a manic-depressive, and I became really very fond of him, even though I seldom saw him in his manic phase. I suppose that my affection for him might be traceable to the fact that my battle with him (I wanted to install one of the two bulk venders I had removed from the Napa poker game) was remarkably bloodless and brief.

"What's that stuff in there?" Joe asked me on the day I put the machine in.

"That's bubble gum, Joe," I said. "Hundred-count bubble gum."

"What's hundred-count mean?"

"A hundred gumballs to the pound, Joe," I replied. Hundred-count gum, incidentally, cost thirty-one cents a pound and brought back one dollar, of which twenty cents went to Joe.

"Is it clean?" he asked.

"The globes are sterilized personally by me and my wife," I replied, "and the gumballs are poured into them from factory-sealed cartons, absolutely untouched by human hands."

Joe nodded up and down and stroked the right side of his mustache with his middle finger.

"I deplore anything unsanitary," Joe said.

"Me, too, Joe," I said. I did not then know how much Joe loved to deplore things.

Well, it didn't take a Gallup Poll among the residents of Frog Hollow to detect a certain coolness toward bubble gum. As a result, at the end of the first month, I took $1.29 out of the machine. No one was happy—not Joe Lopez y Garcia, who got as his share twenty-six cents, nor the customers, nor the poverty-stricken top brass of the Multivend Company.

"I think you better take it out," Lopez y Garcia told me as I handed him two dimes, a nickel, and a penny. "I'm sick-to-death tired of hauling it out to the sidewalk every morning, back inside every night. Out and in, out and in. You take it along with you."

I blanched at the prospect of having to find a new home for the machine. I could just turn it over to Og, of course, as I had originally planned to do anyhow, but it was beginning to look as though Og's relocating program had just been so much Chugwateresque hot air.

"Joe," I said, "the whole problem here is that we just haven't found the right kind of merchandise for this machine. Now I'll tell you what I'm going to do. I'm going to put on some jaw breakers. Everyone's crazy for jaw breakers—you know that!"

"Out and in, out and in," said Joe Lopez y Garcia, shaking his head. "For twenty-six cents a month. I deplore the backache I get. Remove the machine."

"Joe," I said urgently, "I've got an inspiration! What you need is a striped-ball load. Wait—I'll get one from the car and show you."

I dashed out to the Jeep, grabbed a globe of 140-count bubble gum into which Mary-Armour and I, the night before, had carefully loaded twenty-five red-and-yellow-striped gumballs. On the front of the globe a small printed sign proclaimed: "Free 5¢ Candy Bar for Each Striped Ball."

"The kids play it like crazy, see," I said, "trying to get a striped ball. And when they do, you take the striped ball and give the kid any nickel candy bar he wants. Okay?"

"That's really swell," Joe said unenthusiastically. "So then, besides hauling the damn thing back and forth, I'm out a nickel, too, eh? Yeah, that's great—my wife'll go for that!"

"Good Lord, no, Joe!" I said. "You're money ahead! See, you've given out a candy bar that cost you about three cents, and I pay you a nickel for it; I pay you a nickel for each striped ball you've got when I come around. So in addition to your regular 20 per cent commission, you sell a buck and a quarter's worth of candy bars with each globeful of gum!"

"Yeah?" A spark of interest glowed feebly.

"Absolutely!" I said.

The following week, the machine sold out completely. Lopez y Garcia was definitely manic when I arrived to service the machine, and so was I. We took 910 pennies out of the coin box, of which Joe got $1.82 as his regular commission, plus the $1.25 I paid him to redeem the twenty-five striped balls. The merchandise in the globe had cost me $2.03, and my net for the week on that machine, therefore, was exactly $4.00.

Gee whiz, you say, even if the machine only empties one striped-ball load a month, it still earns about a dollar a week! That's right, brother, you're practically quoting Og Chugwater. And if it empties twice a month, it's earning two dollars a week! Amen, brother, you just said a chewy mouthful. And if you had a hundred machines, that would be $200 a week for just two days work! That's entirely correct, brother; you're getting the same fever I had when I started. Care to buy a hundred machines?

The second striped-ball load I put on Lopez y Garcia's machine emptied in two weeks. The third load took a month. The fourth load was only half empty at the end of the following month, and L. y G. was beginning to feel his back pains again.

"You'd better take it along this time," he said. "The poor thing's dying."

"Joe," I told him, as he stood staring morosely at half-empty load number four, "what we need here is a nice, fresh load of Boston Beans."

"I think maybe what we need is for a nice, fresh gum operator to take the machine away," he said.

"Why, Joe," I said reprovingly, "I'm surprised at your

attitude. Why, we've barely scratched the surface here! Don't you remember the time the machine emptied completely in just one week?"

"It did that exactly once," Joe said gloomily. "If there's anything I deplore, it's a flash in the pan."

"Joe," I said, putting my hand dramatically on his shoulder, "this is no flash in the pan. What we've done once, we can do again!" Without waiting for his reply, which I felt might be unsuitable anyway, I went out to the Jeep and brought in a succulent load of Boston Beans. I held the globe aloft for his inspection.

"Shall I put it on?" I said.

"Those are Boston Beans?" he said.

"Correct, Joe," I said.

"They look like pebbles," he said.

"They taste like pebbles, Joe," I said. "Try one."

Joe L. y G. inserted three of the small candies in his mouth. I heard a series of crunching noises and hoped that his bridgework was sturdy.

"It's a peanut inside," he said. "Covered with this brown stuff."

"The brown stuff is alleged to be chocolate, Joe," I explained.

"Why would anyone want to eat these?" he asked.

"You've put your finger right on the crux, Joe," I said. "They don't want to. But look what's mixed in with all the beans."

"You mean them little toys?"

"Precisely," I said. "Charms. The kids go for the charms something terrific. And they get them, too. Of course, they get a hell of a lot of beans along with them. But it brings in the pennies, Joe, and I'm sure it will empty in no time. What do you say, Joe—shall I put this load on?"

"God forgive me," Joe said, grimacing at the ceiling, "but go ahead."

I am happy to say that Joe Lopez y Garcia's first load

of Boston Beans emptied in three days, which is a glorious and fitting tribute not only to J. L. y G.'s vision, but to the pulling power of the tiny metal, wood, and plastic trinkets mixed in with the beans.

The finest Boston Bean recipes that Mary-Armour and I were able to compound called for about a quarter- to a half-pound of charms to be arranged artfully throughout some seven pounds of beans. The resulting mixture was enclosed in a squarish glass globe about the size of your head.

Naturally, we were always very careful to load the charms with the best pulling power right up against the front of the glass globe, where they would serve as visual stimulation to tiny investors, and where no nasty beans would get in their way. The rest of the charms, mostly plastic, we merely stirred into the beans in a large metal mixing pan and then poured into the globe. The sound of these hard-shelled beans trilling out of their cardboard container into the mixing pan, incidentally, always reminded me of the Chopin Etude, Opus 25, Number 6, an elegant observation which is included solely to persuade you that Captain Gumball was not such a bum as you thought.

In our day, Mary-Armour and I loaded these globes with a thousand different kinds of charms, including metal and plastic saddles, cowboy boots, crossed guns, uncrossed guns, banjos, violins, fake coins, wedding bells, airplanes, spacemen, dogs, cats, lions, road signs, harmonicas that actually play two notes (very popular), sailboats, friendship rings, cream pitchers, whistles that whistle, whistles that don't whistle, jackknives that really open, miniature playing cards (one of our hottest items), bowling pins, basketballs and baseballs, loving cups, hot dogs, toilet seats (withdrawn from circulation almost immediately at Mary-Armour's insistence), cigarette packs, authentic foreign stamps rolled up and inserted in capsules, compasses that really point north (as well as several other popular directions), motorcycles, auto wheels, fortune wheels (which, when spun, tell you whether your next sweetheart will be slim, rich, tall or ugly), traffic lights set with red and green stones, metal bracelets enclosed in plastic spheres, devil's heads, lariats, baby carriages, phonograph records, elephants, signal flags, screwballs (a screw attached to a ball, much in demand), lightbulbs alleged to glow in the dark, ships-in-bottles, swans, horseshoes, sirens that blow, maze puzzles, pinball games, pocketbooks, flashlights, license plates, and anything else you'd care to mention.

The only real merchandise dud we handled were chocolate peanuts. These, unlike the pebbly Boston Beans, were a good grade of peanut rolled in a generous coating of delicious high-grade milk chocolate. It makes my mouth water just to think of them—I mean, they were good! The minute I tasted them, I knew that everyone would fall in love with this high-quality merchandise, just as I had, so I quickly bought fifty pounds of them and rushed half a dozen globefuls into circulation.

Within a week I discovered (1) that if the direct sun hit chocolate peanuts, they melted—oh God, they melted! (2) that the milk chocolate was as sensitive as a photographic plate and bleached white in stores with only moderate illumination; (3) that even in stores where the conditions of light, heat, and foot traffic were perfect, chocolate peanuts sold slower than gas heaters in the Congo.

Since most of our merchandise was coated with sugar, we soon found that it was attractive to a wide variety of customers. One night I went to the bedroom we had designated as our "storeroom" and immediately gasped and called for Mary-Armour.

"Sweetie-pie," I chirped, putting little grace notes into my voice. "Sugar plum . . . lover . . . dearest . . ."

Mary-Armour appeared in the door. "What's wrong?" I made a face. "Pismires," I said.

"How perfectly revolting!" Mary-Armour said. "What are pismires?"

"Ants," I answered. "Ants in the Boston Beans."

Mary-Armour struck her forehead. "I suppose they're in everything—the bubble gum and all."

I checked the bubble-gum cartons. "Nope, not in the bubble gum."

"How about the chocolate peanuts?"

I checked again. "Even the ants won't eat chocolate peanuts," I said.

"What'll we do?"

"Well," I said, "have you ever separated whites from yolks? Or men from boys? Or sheep from goats, or shoe-clerks from real gamblers?"

"All of that," Mary-Armour said. "Many's the time."

"Then tonight," I said, "you shall separate ants from Boston Beans!"

We took the ant-ridden carton into the kitchen, got two cookie sheets with turned-up edges, and threw a cupful of Boston Beans on each. Then, by tipping the cookie sheets back and forth and applying a principle known as "Nelson's Theory of Inertia in Pismires" (stated simply: "Ants don't roll"), we soon removed a large number of ants and destroyed them. We also removed any beans that looked gnawed. This process kept our eyeballs spinning till long after midnight.

The following morning we called in a pest-control outfit to antproof our house on a yearly basis. Thereafter, at the first patter of tiny ant feet, we merely telephoned the ant man, who much to our pleasure and surprise, responded immediately with effective counter-measures.

Naturally, a part of the cost of de-anting the place was deductible from Multivend's exceedingly slender income as a business expense. There were a lot of other deductible items, too, like depreciation on the machines and Jeep, meals on the road, bridge tolls going to and from San Francisco for merchandise (we never went to San Francisco that we didn't pick up enough bubble gum to write the trip off as a business expense), part of the house rent, light, telephone, and heat. To keep track of such deductions, we maintained a set of books more minute and complicated than anything kept by General Motors or U.S. Steel. A typical entry read:

April 4	Parking	$ .04	
	Meals (ice-cream cone)	.10	
	Telephone	.10	
	Misc. (doughnut)	.05	
	Cr. Cash		.29

Good Lord, you say, you mean you kept records of such petty stuff as that? Well, the fact was, we were frightened silly that our books might overstate our meager income when income-tax time came around. So we put down every penny we spent, spurred on by the depressing knowledge that to offset an expense of $1, roughly 250 kiddies had to step up to one of our machines, each armed with a penny and the impulse to chew.

I don't really know why that should bring to mind the two recurrent fears that beset me frequently in the morning just as I was starting out for a round of servicing. One fear was that I would find every machine just as full of merchandise as it was when I left it the week before, if not fuller. The other was that I would find every store-keeper in a hideously angry, uncompromising mood, and that they would all tell me to take my machines the hell out of their stores forever. Fortunately, neither fear ever materialized, although the Saga of Bright Oaks Terrace, which I was shortly to experience, shows what can happen to a perfectly innocent gumball magnate like me.

8

There actually came a day when, through the mail, I received a list of the new locations No-Name had scratched up for me. Og's note accompanying the list stated that one of his men had moved the machines only a day or so before, from the old to the new locations. I immediately hopped into the Jeep and took off to see just what kind of job No-Name had done. My first stop was in a place called Bright Oaks Terrace.

Bright Oaks Terrace was (and is, for that matter) a housing development completely devoid of oak trees on the outskirts of one of my chicle metropolises. It was built during World War II, and it consisted of some hundred to two hundred cheaply built but well-maintained houses, an administration building, a grocery store, and an automatic laundry.

There were two other components, I discovered as I

drove through the front gate of the project, that were of great interest to me. One was a large band of penny-clutching kids, and the other was a tall board fence around the perimeter of the development to keep this captive audience from escaping. Actually, since Bright Oaks Terrace was a goodly distance out of the city, there was no particular place to escape to, except possibly to the nearby lumber mill where most of the local fathers worked.

As you can see, Bright Oaks Terrace was a sort of heaven for a gum-machine operator, assuming, of course, that he could place a couple of machines in the area. I feel that it should be marked down to No-Name's everlasting credit, therefore, that one of its geopoliticians managed to land two units in the Bright Oaks Grocery, a middle-sized pineboard operation presided over by a Mr. Primus Gideon and his wife.

As I pulled the Jeep to a halt in front of Gideon's store, I was a trifle dismayed not to see my machines in action anywhere. Perhaps they were inside, I decided. I walked in the front door, looked around, but saw them nowhere. Then I saw Gideon.

Gideon was standing behind the cash register, staring two holes through my head. He was a morose-looking chap, about thirty-eight years old, long and lanky, and sharp of feature. His nose was long and straight, thin enough to cut the finger that was slowly massaging the length of it, up and down, up and down. His dark hair was parted in the middle and plastered down toward his ears. His brow wore a permanent scowl.

"Good morning," I said cheerily.

Gideon nodded up and down. "Good morning," he conceded. He had a delivery that would have done credit to an Old Testament prophet. He had only spoken two words, but he had foretold the end of the world.

A tall redhead, looking like a grim baby doll with highly rouged cheeks, and her hair in ringlets, appeared from the storeroom and stood beside Gideon, looking at me. She turned out to be Gideon's wife, of course, and I imagined that she might have been quite attractive before she achieved co-deaconhood by marrying Gideon.

"My name's Nelson," I said to the two of them. "I'm the gum-machine man, but I don't see the machines. I hope nothing's wrong."

Gideon fixed me with a beady eye. "My friend," he said, carefully eliminating any telltale hint of friendliness from his voice, "the machines are in the back room. You may split up the proceeds with us and then take the machines away forever."

"Take 'em away!" I said indignantly. "Why, they were just put in!"

The warm feeling of outrage left me abruptly, however, as I remembered what the exact business relationship was between mighty Gideon, the storekeeper, and lowly me, the penny-gum man. I put a little Uriah Heep into my act.

"You're the boss," I said, "and what you say goes. But first would you mind telling me what's wrong? I mean, it's my first trip out here, and already I find you want to get rid of me. Maybe—if you tell me—I can fix up whatever's the matter."

"The matter," Gideon proclaimed grandly from his pulpit behind the cash register, "is that your machines are empty. Four days ago your man put them in; two days ago they were empty."

"I get the picture, Mr. Gideon," I said. "Golly, that's terrific, and I don't blame you for being sore that they sat empty a couple of days. 'An empty machine maketh no pelf,' " I added, and was about to attribute the quote to Confucius, but I perceived quickly that the lighthearted approach was not for Gideon. I got serious again, *muy pronto.*

"Why, if I'd known that," I said, "I'd sure have been

here sooner, but you see, I just got notification by mail that they'd been put in. I'll keep them full from now on, though!"

"You have missed the point completely," Gideon orated. "The point is that for two interminable days I had those machines in front of my meat counter, and for two interminable days I had kids fighting right here in the store for the privilege of putting the next penny in the machine. How many pennies are there in those two monsters?"

"Let's see," I said, squinting at the ceiling, "about nine dollars in the ball-gum machine, and eight in the Boston Bean. About seventeen dollars."

"Seventeen dollars," Gideon said. "That's 1,700 pennies that I had to give out to 1,700 kids so that they could stage 1,700 fights over who got to play the machine next. It's driving my legitimate customers away. I can't have it. Take them out of here."

"How about this?" I countered. "We'll put the machines outside the store on the sidewalk. That'll keep the kids out of the store, and at the same time you'll still get your generous commission. Besides, this is just the first load to go through the machine. The whole thing's new, and the kids go for it. As time goes on, they'll settle down and won't fight over it so much."

The deacon considered this proposal while his red-headed wife, ringlets quivering, gave me almost word for word his speech about 1,700 pennies, kids, and fights. Finally Gideon seemed to have made up his mind.

"All right," he said. "We'll try them one more week."

I loaded the machines and set them out in front of the store, while the deacon preached a sermon on *Bakery Ethics, The Absence of,* to the driver of a bread truck, whose misfortune it was to have Bright Oaks Grocery on his route. When I had everything all set, I walked back in and thanked the Gideons for their kind consideration.

Three days later, with apprehension in my bones, I chugged up to the Bright Oaks Grocery on reconnaissance. Once again I found the machines out of sight. Gideon, who was standing behind the meat counter looking like a shirt-sleeved, red-gallused avenging angel, told me they had gone empty the previous evening.

"Your machines are a menace to my business!" he told me. "I have $16,000 invested in this store, and I have better things to do than change nickels, dimes, and quarters into pennies so that kids can play your machines!" Gideon looked at me balefully and branched out into another sermon, this time about the ungrateful operator of the coin laundry.

"I change plenty of paper into silver so the women hereabouts can patronize his laundry," he said, "but do you suppose he ever comes by to see if I'm low on change? No, he does not! He just carries all the silver he takes from those machines right off the project. Well, I can't get rid of him, but I can sure by God get rid of the penny problem! You may take them out," he said, jerking his head toward the back room where my machines reposed, "as soon as we divvy up the money."

I knew I had to fight for time. At the rate the Bright Oaks machines were emptying, it was easily my best location. If I lost it, I'd probably develop some awful neurosis. I threw my heaviest artillery at Gideon.

"Mr. Gideon," I said earnestly, "what if I buy a machine that will change nickels, dimes, and quarters into pennies? Now, I don't even know if such a beast exists, but let me try to find one and install it and save you all that fuss over making change. Then we'll both be happy, right?"

"You can look for such a machine," Gideon said, "but meanwhile get your machines out of here. Furthermore," he added darkly, "I'm not saying for sure I'll let you put them back in, even if you do get a coin changer. We'll just have to see."

Gideon began to sharpen a savage-looking knife as he spoke, and I was relieved to see that it was intended for a hindquarter of beef and not for me. I knew that my cause was lost until I found a penny changer; maybe it was lost even then. So I divided up the pennies, and loaded my machines into the back of the station wagon, and departed.

On my way out of the project I drove up and down all the streets, looking for another spot to locate my machines. The self-service laundry and the post office looked like the only decent spots—short of getting some householder to install a vender on his front porch.

The postmaster regretted that postal regulations said nix on gum machines in post offices. The laundry was so exceedingly self-service that no one was in attendance. I didn't feel I should put my machine on the launderette wall without getting permission from someone, so I went to the administration building, got the name of the San Francisco outfit that operated the laundry (without mentioning why I wanted to know), and went my way. Meanwhile, I fired off a letter to a company with the unlikely name of "National Rejectors, Inc.," to ask about coin changers.

The laundry owner, whom I called on in San Francisco soon thereafter, was a slim, friendly, race-track type in yellow shoes, flannel trousers, dark glasses, and a horse-blanket sport coat. He couldn't have been more agreeable.

"Sure," he told me, as he indolently scratched a molar with a gold toothpick. "Go ahead. Put up as many machines as you want." Then he cocked his head a little to one side and narrowed his eyes, and pumped his eyebrows up and down. For a moment he looked a great deal like Truslow Thomas, only with blood in his veins.

"Incidentally," he said, "how would you like to *buy* that laundry?"

He named some figure which I don't remember, probably because the idea of anyone in my impoverished condition buying anything at all struck me as so hilarious. I told him no thanks on the laundry purchase, and then, in a low voice which I almost hoped he wouldn't hear, I said it was customary for the poor blokes who operated gum machines to pay out some sort of commission to the owner of the location.

The king of the coin laundries waved his hand regally. "Forget it," he said. I kissed the hem of his sport coat and crawled out the door on my hands and knees.

The following morning I Jeeped up to the laundry, bristling with screwdrivers, pliers, hammers, and other carpentering paraphernalia. I picked out a good spot on the side of the building—out of the rain, yet easily accessible—and began to attach a bracket to the wall. Within seconds I had fifteen children breathing down my neck, fingering my tools, offering helpful hints, and asking questions, the most popular of which was "can we have some gum, mister?"

I held off on the free samples until the machine was actually fastened to the wall. Then, to celebrate the opening of this great new chicle emporium, I distributed one stick of Juicy Fruit to each child present.

The effect was electric. Within half a minute the crowd had tripled in size. It was still swelling as I hastily collected my tools and, scattering gum like rose petals, started my escape. As I drove off, I noted cheerfully that some of the children were already inserting their pennies in the machine. I felt smug as a bug in a mink rug.

A few days later, when I returned to service the machine, I found it two-thirds empty. It probably would have been completely drained if someone hadn't jammed it by putting a piece of gum in the coin slot. I cleared the jam, reloaded the machine, and went my way.

The next time I returned, the machine was half-empty and jammed. I rather suspected the deacon as the guilty party, but naturally I was topheavy with prejudice. Even with the jamming, however, the machine was doing a nice business, and I decided that the next time I came I would put up a second machine.

Partly because I remembered Gideon's sermon about the ungrateful laundryman, and partly because I wanted to see how the old boy was taking it, I cruised over to his store and strolled in.

Gideon immediately stopped lecturing a cowed and be-wildered rack jobber who had stumbled unawares into the store, and turned to me. His brow darkened like a storm over the Dead Sea. His wife glowered as best she could, but her effort came nowhere near matching Gideon's superb cloud effects.

"You!" Gideon barked at me. "I'd like to tell you how many kinds of s.o.b. we've called you this past week!"

"We're *mad* at you!" his wife chimed in.

Will anyone blame me if I felt all warm and rosy inside?

"I just thought you might want some pennies," I said. "I remembered what you told me about the laundryman."

Gideon picked up a meat cleaver and hacked savagely at a saddle of lamb.

"Do you know who has to supply all those pennies for your machine?" he demanded.

Naturally I knew.

"That's why I'm here," I said. "Listen, don't get sore, Mr. Gideon—I'm just trying to be friendly. I just thought your penny supply might be getting low." I was engulfed in a sort of three-martini glow.

"I'll tell you who supplies the pennies!" Gideon orated,

ignoring my remarks. "WE supply them, that's who!"
Hack! went the cleaver! I began to worry a bit about
Gideon's fingers.

"We have just as many kids in here as when we had the
machines!" he said. (Hack!) "And when I try not giving
the kids change, (hack!) their parents hop down my
throat— 'How come you won't give my kid (hack!) five
pennies (hack!) for a nickel?' " (Hack! Hack! Hack!)

My mind was reeling with joy, but I tried to remain
outwardly sober.

"We might as well have your monsters back here and
get our percentage as have them up there!" Gideon
fumed.

I longed to tell him that I wasn't paying any percentage
at the laundry, but I saw no reason to get him any angrier.

"You can have them back here if you want," I said.

"No!" Gideon thundered. He raised the cleaver and
pointed it at me. "Listen, your machines are portable—
my grocery isn't. Why don't you just take them out of
Bright Oaks Terrace altogether?"

"Because it's a good location," I said, "and because I
have to make a living, the same as you."

"Says who?" Gideon snapped. There was a pause while
Gideon and I stared at one another.

"Well," I said, "I guess you don't want any pennies
then, do you."

"I never want to *see* a penny again!" Gideon said. "And
if these kids keep on pestering me for pennies, I'll take the
matter up with the administration office!"

I had been afraid of this. And sure enough, the next
time I came by, my machine was missing from the laundry
wall. I went straight to the administration building, ready
to give up without a struggle. All I wanted was my machine back.

The Big Boss of the project was waiting for me, all
geared up for an argument. When he learned that I only

wanted my machine, and not a round or two of fisticuffs, he calmed down considerably. He even went so far as to say he was sorry—sorry that permission to operate gum machines wasn't specifically written into the laundry's lease. We shook hands, and I walked out, sad in the knowledge that I was being exiled from Bright Oaks Terrace— at least until the grocery changed hands.

As I drove the Jeep up the winding asphalt road to the project exit, I took one last longing look at the hordes of children swarming over the lawns, stampeding around the houses. I felt like Adam being cast out of Eden.

9

It took a while for Mary-Armour and me to recuperate from the cruel blow Primus Gideon had struck. But our recovery was aided immensely by the fact that the rains ended suddenly and irrevocably, and spring began to bust out all over. Mary-Armour and I discovered that, no matter what other follies we might have committed, we'd made at least one intelligent decision—to live in Sonoma County.

Almost overnight the brown hills on either side of our valley disappeared completely. They were green hills now. There were blossoms everywhere, a thousand varieties of wildflowers, bushes, trees. Every country road, every street in a town, every inch of pasture put on its own special color. Young fruit trees that had looked like skinny sticks stuck in the ground all winter were furred over-night with fragile blossoms—pink, magenta, cerise, white. Intricate yellow flowers with delicate black traceries turned whole meadows into a sea of saffron, right up to the edge of the road. The air was soft, the sun was warm, and the traffic in seed catalogues was something fearful.

"Now that spring is here," Mary-Armour said, as we lay in bed early one cool morning, staring at the patterns of sunlight on the bedroom wall and listening to the early birds discussing worms outside our window, "we ought to get a dog."

"I'm all in favor of getting a dog," I said, "but what has spring got to do with it?"

"You have to housebreak dogs, darling," Mary-Armour said, "and nobody would want to put a tiny puppy out in the winter rain."

Mary-Armour's thoughts must have been telepathic, because two days later my pint-size friend, Freddie Wing Duck, offered me a dog, absolutely free.

"Very fine dog," Freddie said. He was standing behind the cash register, his fingers wandering nervously over the keys as though they were seeking The Lost Chord.

"Part German shepherd," he amplified. "You follow, I show you."

I followed Freddie through the back of his store, past a vegetable sink where the shapely Moonstone was trimming lettuce and cabbages, out into a fenced-in dirt backyard littered with hundreds of empty cardboard cartons and wooden crates. At one side of the yard, stretched at full length on the bare earth, was a large, suspicious-looking German shepherd dog feeding five of the largest, furriest puppies I had ever seen.

"You stay back," Freddie said. "She know me."

He walked over to the dog, patted her on the head, and disconnected a tremendous, dark-gray puppy, which he brought over to me.

"This best one," Freddie said, holding the puppy up for my inspection. "Good dog. One-half part German shepherd."

"What's the other half?" I said.

Freddie shrugged his shoulders. "Lots of dogs in this neighborhood," he said. He put the puppy in my hands. "You want this one? Lady dog."

The puppy looked up at me and wagged her tail, and then, although it was not strictly necessary, as I was already eager to become her owner, she licked my hand. I held her up to eye level and looked into her round brown eyes, and I knew immediately that she was the dog Mary-Armour had been talking about two days earlier.

Freddie found a box for the pup to travel in, and I thanked him profusely for both dog and box. As a parting question, I asked him what the puppy ate.

Freddie gave a quick, insouciant shrug and began to twirl his long key chain.

"Milk good to start," he said. "After that, noodles, bean sprouts, anything."

Despite Mary-Armour's charge that I had been given a full-grown dog instead of a puppy, the pup was an instant success at home. She scrambled around the kitchen floor, puddling and falling down with about equal frequency. Jamie, who could walk pretty well now, followed her everywhere, trying vainly to pick her up and carry her. He'd never seen a dog up close before, and he was enchanted. For no very good reason that I can remember, Mary-Armour suggested that we name the dog Cleopatra, which we did, and within the matter of a few bright spring days, Cleo was as much a member of the family as Mommy or Daddy or Jamie.

We hoped, of course, that spring would breathe new life into the Multivend Company. We knew it meant the end of machines fouled up by the rain, but we also hoped it might mean a pickup in sales, and the beginning of something we kept referring to vaguely as "normal operations." We knew that if "normal operations" didn't set in soon, we'd really be in trouble, because our bank account, which had received such a rich transfusion when we sold the truck, had already nosedived alarmingly.

The fact that the first collection following the end of the rains was within fifteen cents of the preceding month's total (and fifteen cents *less*, at that) didn't bother us at all. We knew that the pennies being collected during that first spring month had been earned during the rains. It would be the *next* month's collections that would show the upsurge. So we settled back and watched the roses grow—our place was alive with them—and watched Jamie and Cleo the puppy grow, too.

Of the two, Cleo grew the faster. I don't know how she would have done on noodles and bean sprouts, but on table scraps, kibbled dog meal, milk, and occasional horse-meat, it seemed as though she grew a pound a day. Mary-Armour was sure that the unknown dog that had sired her had been a St. Bernard, and as the days wore on, she revised her guess to Shetland pony.

And then, one sunny Wednesday morning, it was time to collect the month's pennies. Reluctantly I laid aside the short story I had begun two days before—I'd decided to have a go at story writing when the pottery vase I was making developed a crack—and prepared to spend the next three or four days on the road, draining coppers from our machines.

I was up by 6:30, breakfasted by 7:15. Then, tripping constantly over Cleo, who wanted to chase my shoes and snap at them, and Jamie, who wanted to chase Cleo and snap at her, I began to assemble my equipment. First I picked up from the kitchen floor a box containing six freshly filled glass globes (Mary-Armour and I had loaded them the night before) and carried them outdoors to the Jeep. I laid them gently on the floor of the car and went back for another of the two remaining boxes. I found Jamie looking like a squirrel, with a gumball in each cheek, his mouth covered with red and blue vegetable dye.

He was rolling gumballs across the kitchen floor, and Cleo was chasing them. I emptied Jamie's mouth and put him in the playpen to keep him out of the way, and then I emptied Cleo's mouth and put her in the playpen, too.

Then Mary-Armour took my plywood gum carrier out to the car (it was a flat, home-made, rectangular box with a removable front, that held 1,900 sticks of gum in ten tall columns), and I followed with a carton containing fifty extra boxes of tab gum. Next, with a check-off list in my hand, I assembled a pair of pliers; a screwdriver; an ice pick; a metal punch; my route cards; my receipt book; the penny scale; a large, shapeless brown traveling bag to hold the pennies I collected; the keys to the machines (twice, before I initiated the routine of the check-off list, I drove thirty miles to my first stop before realizing I'd left the keys at home); two diapers, one for cleaning machines, the other for polishing; a can of auto polish, for use with the diapers; extra stickers for pasting on striped-ball globes; a pack of self-addressed stamped post cards to give to locations so that when something went wrong they could drop one in the mail to me (instead of phoning collect, as they usually did); and finally, a pill bottle full of thumbtacks—so the storekeeper could tack the post card up in the store and keep it from getting lost.

I was now ready to go. I kissed Mary-Armour, kissed our gumball-stained son, drew in a deep breath of Sonoma County air, and set out.

Fifteen miles later, at 8:31, I stopped at the Dome Café. I collected $2.78 from the tab-gum machine, which had done only $2.19 the preceding month. At Fran and Jerry's Drive-Inn, I took $4.03 out of a machine which, the month before, had done $3.99. At Perotti's Drugstore, the machine yielded $3.10 as against the preceding month's $2.88.

I felt an elation building up inside me. There *was* a spring upturn in business! It was a very tiny upturn, to be sure, the kind that might expire if you breathed on it too hard, but still, it was progress in the right direction. It was an omen, I felt, a straw in the wind, a weathervane pointing toward the eventual accumulation of immense wealth.

I was whistling as I entered my fourth stop, Hale's Market. I called out cheerily to the portly proprietress.

"Good morning, Mrs. Throg." (There hadn't been a Hale in Hale's Market for twenty years.)

Mrs. Throg regarded me warily and gingerly patted her untidy gray haystack of hair, as though she were searching for a needle.

"What are you so happy about?" she said.

"Everything," I said.

I opened the tab-gum machine, leaned the plywood gum-loader up against it and removed the front. I reloaded with speed and efficiency. I closed the gum-loader, set it aside, and put a fresh globe of Boston Beans on the bulk vender. I polished both machines till they shone. Then I got out a black box containing my spring-type penny scale, adjusted the dial to zero, and emptied a coin box full of pennies onto it. I read from the dial that there was $4.72 in that machine. I dumped the pennies into the brown traveling bag, and then poured the contents of the second coin box onto the scale. The dial showed $5.78. I dumped this second batch of pennies into the traveling bag, recorded the total of $10.50 on my route card, noted happily that the preceding month's total had been only $9.62, and made out a receipt for Mrs. Throg.

I looked to see where she was. As usual, when I wanted to pay her, she was engaged in an interminable conversation with an elderly female customer.

"So I told her," I could hear her say, "that if she was going to treat my very own sister-in-law's niece's son like that . . ."

The customer shook her head sadly, agreeing.

I took out my pocketknife and felt the blade. Better sharpen it when I got home, I decided. I put it back in my pocket and made a few extra passes with the diaper at the already-gleaming machines. I picked up a penny from the traveling bag and flipped it twenty times. It came up heads twelve times, tails eight.

Mrs. Throg's voice rose indignantly: ". . . chasin' after riff-raff! Why, that woman—I know this for a fact, Hilda —that woman . . ."

I took the polishing cloth and rubbed the toes of my scuffed shoes. It didn't do much good. I checked my route cards to make sure they were in the right order for the rest of the day's stops. I looked at Mrs. Throg and decided her hair wasn't a haystack after all. It was a bird's nest. I squinted my eyes half shut and pictured three eggs resting squarely on top of her head, with a seagull just lighting on them.

I wound my wrist watch. I tried holding my breath for as long as I could. I did forty-one seconds. Then I did fifty-two seconds. I decided to see if I could hold it a whole minute.

And then suddenly Mrs. Throg was standing across the counter from me.

"Well," she said, "how much do I get?"

I exhaled explosively. "Two dollars," I said, puffing, "and ten cents. We did pretty well this month."

"*You* did pretty well, you mean," she said. "Two-ten ain't much of a cut, I can tell you that!"

"It's a lot when you think that you didn't have to do anything to get it," I said. "Or spend anything, either, or . . ."

"All right, all right," she said. "Can the sales talk. Just gimme the money. In pennies."

I checked the adjustment of the scale carefully a second time, weighed out $2.10, and handed it to her in the aluminum weighing pan. She stared at it stonily.

"How much is that?" she said.

"That's $2.10," I said.

"Exactly?"

"Well, within a penny either way," I said. "It's either $2.09 or $2.10 or $2.11."

"How do you know that?"

"That's what the scale says."

"Bet it ain't right."

"What do you want to bet?"

"Double or nothing," Mrs. Throg said, "that it ain't two-nine, two-ten, or two-eleven."

"Mrs. Throg," I said, "you've got yourself a bet."

I dumped the pennies on the counter, and she began to arrange them in piles of ten. It took about five minutes, because she counted each pile twice, apparently not satisfied with her first count.

"Well, I'll be!" she said finally. "It's $2.10, right on the nose!"

I smiled indulgently and began to reach for the pennies.

"Whoa, there! What you doin'?" Mrs. Throg said.

My hands paused in mid-air. "What's wrong?"

"You *won*, didn't you?"

"That's right," I said.

"You lucky stiff!" she said. "So you get out of payin' me double, don't you."

"Not only that," I said, "I—"

"All you owe me is this here $2.10," Mrs. Throg said. She scooped the pennies up quickly and dumped them into her cash register. "You lucky stiff!"

I straightened up and stared into the cold gray eyes peering at me from beneath the bird's nest. But Mrs. Throg's store was one of my good locations, so I decided that I might as well not labor the point. I picked up my equipment and headed for the door.

"Well, better luck next time," I said.

Mrs. Throg was bubbling over with good nature. "Oh,

fergit it," she said. "I don't mind losin' a bet now and then."

I stopped next at a pool-and-pinball parlor known as The Black Friday. I found Abel Krotna, the bald, bearded proprietor, shooting a friendly game of pool with the wispy tailor whose shop was next door. Abel's great bulk was spread out nearly horizontal on the table; he was trying to make a centerline shot. One foot was on the floor, and the other lay along the table rail.

"Watch out you don't move something with your goddam whiskers!" the tailor said.

Abel tried the shot, made it, and snorted approvingly at his own skill. Then he saw me.

"Hi. Gotny puzzles?"

"Got one here somewhere," I said. I set my equipment on the floor and began to search the pockets of my coat. "Here it is." I held out the crossword puzzle from the Sunday edition of the New York *Times*, which a kind relative sent us each week by mail. Abel left the game and came over to accept the puzzle.

"Thanks," he said. He scratched his beard meditatively with a match stick and watched me open the machine. "Say, that puzzle last week was a real killer, eh? All that opera stuff. Jeez, I nearly busted my pick on that one!"

"Well, you've got the solution right there," I said. "In this week's paper. You can check and see how well you did."

Abel shook his head and made a face. "Nah, I never check 'em," he said. "It don't seem sportsmanlike."

"What do you mean, not sportsmanlike?"

"It's like usin' a crib when you was in school," he explained. "It ain't honest."

"I never thought of it exactly that way before," I said, "but I suppose you do have a point."

"Yeah," Abel said. He headed back toward the brightly

lit green rectangle in the dark rear of his store and began chalking his cue. "Tell you something else," he said over his shoulder. "In all the years I been doin' puzzles, I never yet left a space blank."

"There aren't many men who can say that," I said. I watched Abel sight his shot.

"Darn tootin' there ain't!" he said.

"I guess that's how we get new words in the language," I said.

Abel paused in his sighting, looked up at me measuringly for a moment, as though trying to sniff out any disrespect in my remark. Apparently he found none, for he bent over his cue again and slammed the six-ball into the side pocket.

At my next stop I handed over four rolls of white pennies—the wartime substitute for copper cents—and received two one-dollar bills in return from Jelke Fitzgibbon, the proprietor. One of Jelke's elderly lady customers was collecting the white coins, and through me, he was helping her out.

Freddie Wing Duck's was my next stop, and I was glad to note that Freddie had achieved at least a partial solution to the problem of his excess nervous energy. He had bought a Bongo Board. A Bongo Board, in case you've never seen one (this was my first), consists of a wooden cylinder about six or eight inches in diameter, and a rectangular board. The trick is to put the board on top of the cylinder and then stand on the board, with one foot at either end. By shifting your weight—if you're any good —you can make the cylinder roll back and forth. If you're not any good, the cylinder rolls suddenly, the board slips out from under you, and you end up with both legs in traction.

Freddie was good. He stood astride his Bongo Board, making it go from side to side behind the cash register, with his hands in his pockets. Besides giving him an outlet for his energies, it added six much-needed inches to his height. In all the weeks I'd been there I'd never seen him look happier.

"How's the dog?" Freddie asked, only in Freddie's percussive jargon it sounded like "Hozza dok?"

"She's fine, Freddie," I said. "Big as a house. My wife and I certainly appreciate your giving her to us."

"Sure. Have cup coffee."

"Wish I could, Freddie," I said. "But I haven't got time today."

Freddie shrugged and went on Bongo-ing.

"That's a pretty fine device you've got there," I said. "Where'd you get it?"

"Uncle send from Chicago," Freddie said. "Have fortune cookie?" Still rolling back and forth, he reached under the counter and brought out the cookie sack. I took one, thanked him, opened it, and withdrew the tiny slip of paper.

" 'So sorry,' " I read aloud, " 'Man who tell fortune— he sick.' "

"Ho-ho-ho-ho-ha-ha-ha-ha!" Freddie laughed, nearly falling off the Bongo Board. "Big joke! I buy in city."

My next stop was in the Skid Row section of town at a place noted down on my route card simply as Ben's. Its real name, however, was The Grand National Shoe-Shining Parlor. It could afford such a luxurious title, because it was a two-chair stand.

The proprietor, Ben Thurlow, was just opening up as I pulled my gumball-laden Jeep to the curb in front of his stand.

"Good morning, Ben," I said. He looked up quickly and smiled.

"Good morning, Mr. Nelson," he said. Ben was one of the very few people on the route who remembered my name, and the only one who called me "mister." Ben was fifteen years old, a sophomore in high school, and a real entrepreneur. He stood about five-feet-ten, had blue eyes and blond hair, appropriately crew cut. He fairly radiated potential energy.

Ordinarily Ben didn't appear at the stand until three o'clock, at which time, usually accompanied by an admiring employee his own age, he would be open for business. For several hours the stand would be surrounded by at least half a dozen boys, one of whom might even have enough spare cash to indulge in the luxury of a shine. The rest, however, just hung around. They talked some, and they watched adults getting their shoes shined (where customers came from in that crummy section of town, I never quite understood), and they listened to Ben hold forth on a variety of subjects. Occasionally they dropped a few pennies into the tab-gum machine that was fastened to the exterior wall of Ben's tiny stand. Ben's cut was a standard 15 per cent, which I ordinarily sent him by mail.

"How come you're here this morning?" I asked. "I thought you'd be in school."

"I got special permission," he said. "I'm taking inventory."

While I serviced the machine and removed the pennies, Ben went on counting up large stacks of off-brand razor blades, shoe laces, cards of dime novelties, etc. He sold all these things at severely slashed prices, having picked them up from distressed sources known only to himself.

In addition to Ben's activities of shoe-shining and merchandising, he edited and published a weekly newspaper of about eight pages, mimeographed, which usually featured as its front-page story an attack on corruption in local city politics, a subject on which Ben seemed to be exceptionally well informed. The paper had 130 paid subscribers, many of whom held down minor jobs in the city courthouse and whose papers were delivered only after it had been ascertained that their corrupt bosses were off somewhere in their Cadillacs. The remainder of the paper was given over to a few paid advertisements and a great number of feature stories, including in a typical issue a story pointing out the greatness of Lincoln, advice on gardening (written in such telegraphic prose that one paragraph could convey a whole gardenful of information: "Plant corn now. Trim box hedges. Fertilize roses, spray for aphids . . .") and a column entitled simply, "Jokes about Doctors." The other articles would be equally pithy, and there was always an editorial suggesting some civic improvement, such as the creation of a clubhouse for old people, some place they could come to play chess, talk, and enjoy light refreshments.

I weighed out the pennies and grinned at Ben. "Three-fifteen in it this month," I said.

"Gee, that's good," Ben said. "Last month it only had $2.87."

I verified the sum on my card. "You've got a good memory," I said. "Now let's see how good you are with figures. Quick, what's 15 per cent of $3.15?"

Ben sucked in his lower lip and looked thoughtful.

"Point-four-seven-two-five," he said.

"God help your competition!" I said, and handed him forty-eight cents.

On the edge of town I picked up a hitchhiker. I had a rule against hitchhikers, but this one didn't look very dangerous. He was a tired-looking man about seventy with a finely drawn face and a white mustache. He could have been a Confederate cavalry general.

"Now, I'll give you my bus ticket," he said, as we started up. "I have a bus ticket, you know, but I couldn't wait for the bus. You can cash it in Santa Rosa and get some money."

"Thanks," I said. "You keep it."

"It would oblige me if you took it, sir," he said.

"Thanks, I wouldn't have any use for it."

"If you'd rather," the old man said, "I'll fix a gun for you sometime instead."

He gave me his address and urged me to bring him a gun—any kind of gun—and he'd fix it. He was, he confided, sick in the head occasionally and couldn't hold down a regular job, but he had a cabin on a prune ranch up the valley, where in exchange for doing chores when he was able, the rancher gave him food and lodging. He had a small pension from an eastern utility company, and guns had been his lifelong hobby, although he no longer had any guns, just his tools.

He rode with me as far as Sebastopol, which was the only town on the route—and perhaps in all the United States—where the logging trains ran right down the middle of the main street.

When I finished servicing and collecting in Sebastopol (it didn't take long; I only had three machines there), I set out for the next town. This town was also unique, in its own way, for while it had no logging trains, it did have a lady pool-hall operator. The lady was young and attractive and pleasant and played a fair game of pool and was, for a time, married to the man who operated the bar next door. This would seem to be an unbeatable package deal. But, as a friend explained to me, she was Aries and he was Capricorn, so obviously it just couldn't work out.

The two of them remained friendly, though, even while they were getting the divorce, and I used to see Aries sitting on a stool in Capricorn's bar long after she'd got back from Reno. I used to wonder, now that they were no longer man and wife, if he made her start paying for her drinks.

I serviced the lady pool-hall operator's machine, found that it had done fifty-four cents less than the preceding month, and then headed for Henry Skill's supermarket.

I always approached Henry's market with apprehension, because Henry was not exactly the jolly, friendly type. He was a small, shifty-eyed man, the kind you might draw in India ink with thin, nervous lines and no shading. He had moved to California from the Bronx, and although he had made the switch from collars and ties to sport shirts, he had never been able to give up vests. It always came as a visual shock to see his brownish pepper-and-salt vest (no coat, of course) worn over an orange sport shirt covered with undulating hula dancers.

Skill's head was completely bare of any foliage except for a small equatorial fringe and a long inch-wide strand of black hair that originated in the vicinity of one ear (I was never sure which one) and proceeded straight across his north pole to the other ear. The first time I saw Skill, I thought he had been wearing earphones and had forgotten to remove the headband. I remember also that I thought he was winking at me (he had a tic in his left eye), and all in the spirit of friendliness I winked back, which made him furious and started our relationship off on the wrong foot. By the time I approached him a few weeks later with a line of I-hear-you're-from-New-York-too, the only response he would offer was a sneer and the question, "Yeah? So who told you?"

On the day in question, Skill's nerves, always edgy, had been ground down finer than Excalibur. He slashed at me the minute I walked in the door.

"Take 'em out!" he barked, referring to my two machines. "I hate these fast deals!"

The source of the trouble was commissions. Skill claimed No-Name had promised him a straight 25 per cent on both machines. I was giving him 25 per cent on the bulk, but only 15 per cent on the tab gum. Skill snarled at me and breathed fire.

"Gee whiz, Mr. Skill," I said, "I assure you I knew nothing about that. I've been going by the percentages on this card that No-Name gave me, and they listed you at fifteen per cent and twenty-five per cent."

Skill screwed his face into a purple leer. His left eye was winking twice a second. "Take 'em out!" he snapped angrily.

Nobody, but nobody, hates to grovel more than I, especially when the grovelee is someone like Henry Skill. But Henry's supermarket was one of my better locations, and I didn't want to lose it. So I groveled.

"Let me do this, Mr. Skill," I said, in my most humble, reformed-sinner tone of voice. "Let me dip back into the records and refigure the percentages, and pay you the difference between what you actually got and what you should have got. From now on the commission will be a straight twenty-five per cent. But please, please don't throw me out because of a completely unintentional misunderstanding."

Skill lowered the voltage on his leer, transforming it into a sneer. It was easy to see that his frustrations were letting up on him, one by one. He smoothed his narrow band of hair with the palm of his hand. I could sense his knotted intestinal tract relaxing. I could almost hear his ulcer settle back and say, "Oh, well, I've given the old boy enough for one day."

"All right," Skill growled. "Pay the checkout girl." Then he turned and walked away, majestic in triumph. It's always nice to have a psychological whipping-boy around, and the penny-gum man is ideal for this purpose. I know I was very therapeutic for him.

Walking out of Skill's store, I found it hard to make up my mind about the day. Skill had shaken me badly. Still, his ulcer had been propitiated, and my machines still remained in his store. And besides, I had to admit that I was collecting more pennies this month than I had collected in the brief history of the route.

Something going on in my own stomach made me look at my watch. It was twelve-fifteen, and I was hungry. I called on my last stop in Skill's town, collected $3.51 from the gum machine there, bought a quart of milk, and headed out of town.

A mile or so out of town the road passed between two large fields of stubby, rugged-looking plants laid out in regular rows. A year before I wouldn't have known what they were. This was because I had always envisioned a vineyard as a multiplication of those large latticed structures that supported Concord grapes in the backyards of Denver, Colorado, where I grew up. Whenever I read in books about French vineyards, I immediately got a picture of hillsides covered with thousands of these lath arbors, with picturesque peasants walking hand-in-hand beneath them.

Now, of course, I knew better. I even knew that if a California vineyard is owned by someone fairly new to the business, it's not a vineyard at all. It's a grape ranch.

Should I eat in the vineyard? Nope, no shade. I drove on.

Twenty minutes later I climbed out of vineyard country into an area of small mountains. As I crossed a small, clear creek, I considered pulling my station wagon to a halt beside it and lunching under the tall oak trees. I knew from past experience that there would be plenty to keep me interested while I ate—wildflowers, bugs, lizards, fish wriggling lazily through the burbling water, hawks circling overhead. But I had eaten here only a week before. I wanted to break new ground. I pushed on.

At last I came to the sideroad that had been in the back of my mind all along. I turned off the winding highway and started to follow a dirt road that plunged almost straight down a steep hill. At the bottom of the hill, the road turned sharply to the left and disappeared into dense shadow under a tunnel of trees. A quarter of a mile later it emerged into a tiny valley, loaded to the guns with prune trees in full blossom.

I parked the Jeep off the road, leaned my plywood gum-loader against a tree to serve as a backrest, spread my old Navy raincoat on the ground, and sat down. The air smelled rich and earthy. The only noises I heard were the buzz and hum of insects, and the occasional whir of the breeze through the tree boughs. The dappled sunshine warmed my legs; the breeze kept me from getting too hot. I opened a paper sack and withdrew the sumptuous peanut-butter-and-jam sandwich prepared for me by the lovely Chairman of the Board. The cool milk washed easily down my throat between bites. I was at peace with the world. I couldn't even have told you who Henry Skill was.

I opened my paperback novel and began to read. Ten pages, fifteen . . . I found I was reading the same page a third time. I laid the book aside, stretched out full length on my back in the speckled sunlight, and looked up at the quivering white prune blossoms.

The thought flashed through my mind suddenly that I *could*, at that very moment, have been lunching at Twenty-One or Toots Shor's—and with a press agent picking up the tab. Hah, I thought as the prune blossoms flickered dreamily overhead, not this chicken!

But the thought wouldn't go away. "Why not?" it kept saying. "You used to be pretty fond of that routine!"

It was true. Was I kidding myself? Hungrily my mind ran back to the two martinis, the eggs Benedict, the chocolate graham-cracker pie. I thought fondly of the many press agents who had become good friends. In fact, if I was going to be honest with myself, I would have to admit that during the past few months there had been several times when I had longed rather intensely to be back in that warm womb of a good job and a good New York restaurant. Those were the times, of course, when I had to go about my gumball chores in boots and slicker, when merchants left machines out in the rain, when gum melted by the ton. On those soggy days I would gladly have accepted Twenty-One (go ahead, son, *be* a martyr) and the press agent's blandishments, and the expense-account ride across town in the snug taxi.

A cock pheasant strutted into view, not fifteen feet from where I sat, jolting me back into the present. The bird eyed me regally for a moment, and then as the wind rustled one of my sandwich papers, took off vertically in a blur of noise and iridescence.

My troubled thoughts of the life left behind in New York vanished with the bird. Smiling to myself, I lay down again, this time on my stomach, and pillowed my head on my arms. As the sun's delicious warmth penetrated my khaki shirt and trousers, I realized serenely that, while winter was a special case, there would never really be any doubt about the best place in the U.S.A. to eat lunch the rest of the year. While the sun was shining, a prune orchard would always win, hands down.

With a start I suddenly realized I'd dozed off. I looked at my watch. Quarter till two. I yawned once or twice, stood up, stretched, picked up my sandwich papers and the empty milk carton, loaded my equipment into the car, and started back toward the main highway.

Seven miles out of Santa Rosa, I saw an overall-clad man waving a red flag. I pulled to a stop and stuck my head out the window. The flagman, a heavy-set, amiable-looking old gent in a sweat-stained felt hat and dark glasses, approached my car. He was a giant of a man—a size 48 in size 60 overalls—already brown from the spring sun.

"You're just too late," he said. "One-way traffic. Now it's their turn to come from that end for a while."

I shut off my engine.

"Like the feller said," the flagman continued, "might as well relax and enjoy it, eh?"

"You're absolutely right," I said. "Have a stick of gum."

The flagman shook his head. "Can't, thanks. Got false choppers. Sticks to 'em."

"Have a hard candy then."

"Yeah? Don't mind if I do." He took a candy, waved his flag languidly at a pickup truck pulling to a halt behind my Jeep, and turned his attention back to me.

"Real California weather, ain't it?" he said.

I agreed, not realizing at first that this was merely a preamble to his prepared text. He didn't waste any time coming to the point, however—I guess he could never be sure when the traffic would come through from the other way, and he'd have to turn his captive audience loose.

"Yep, wonderful weather," he said, nodding up and down. "Good for a man. Take me, for example."

I smiled. "What about you?" I said.

"Well, sir," he said, drawing in a deep breath, "the Army left me out here in nineteen-and-nineteen—thought it was the only place I'd survive, and at that they told me I couldn't make it past '23. Heart trouble I had, three times, and the flu in '18. They had me all laid out, I want you to know, took me to the morgue and everything."

"Good Lord!" I said. "They took you to the morgue?"

The flagman let out a snort of indignation.

"Yes sir, right there on that marble slab, that's where they had me. That's where I come back to my senses, lyin' there with all them stiffs. And don't think *that* ain't some sensation!"

I shook my head. "Have another candy."

"Yeah. Thanks. Neck was bad, too, you know—not broke exactly, but one of these here vertebraes got dislocated about an inch."

"An inch?"

"Yes, sir, an inch. Maybe more. They told me they couldn't do nothin' about it. Said I'd just have to go ahead and die. But that idea didn't appeal to me none."

"So what did you do?"

"Got me a job workin' outdoors in the sunshine. Light work—flag jobs mostly, like this one. Made enough in the warm months to carry me through the rains without workin'. Been at it thirty-odd years now. Oh, I fooled them Army doctors plenty!"

Just then the traffic started coming through from the other end of the detour. The cars streamed by our stationary column, and the dust from the detour blew slowly into an orchard nearby. Finally the last oncoming car slowed; the driver stuck his arm out the window and handed the flagman a piece of wood with a shredded red rag nailed to it. The flagman signaled to me.

"Take it easy now," he said. "Thanks for the candy."

I started up and left him standing there in the hot sunshine, a living monument to himself and his triumph over enough ailments to finish a dozen ordinary men. (When you come to think of it, the number of sailors and soldiers who have triumphed over Armed Service diagnosticians must be countless!)

About the middle of the afternoon I reached the Frog Hollow Delicatessen and my friend Joe Lopez y Garcia. His store was empty, and I found Joe sitting on a packing box behind the cash register, fanning himself with a newspaper.

"Joe," I said. "You shaved off your mustache!"

"Yeah," he said gloomily.

"How come?"

"It wasn't sanitary," he said.

I shrugged and tried to look impartial.

"Besides, my wife didn't like it," Joe added. He leaned back against a shelf of cigarettes and razor blades, and crossed his legs, wiggling his brown toes through the end of his *huaraches*.

"You know what I deplore more than anything?" he said. "In the sanitary line, that is?"

"What's that, Joe?"

"Washroom doors. In filling stations, restaurants—everywhere."

"What's wrong with washroom doors?" I asked obligingly.

"They open *in*. You come into the washroom, and you do whatever you come in for, and then you wash your hands, and if you're lucky you wipe them on a paper towel. And then you gotta put your nice clean hand on the goddam dirty doorknob to get out!"

"I never thought of that, Joe," I said.

"Nobody ever thinks of it!" Joe said heatedly. "And as a result, every goddam washroom door in America opens *in!*" He stood up and looked me straight in the eye. "I deplore the hell out of it!" he said.

Half an hour later I collected from two machines in a grocery run by Tanaka Watanabe, a courteous Japanese-American. He was assisted in this task by his pretty, giggling, bobby-soxed granddaughter whose name was Mary-Lou. Mr. Watanabe was small, gray, wizened, and immensely dignified. His clothes were always exceptionally neat—starched khaki pants, khaki shirt, black necktie, and a starched white cotton coat. Most of his sentences began with the words "thank you very much" and a slight bow.

"You look a little tired, Mr. Watanabe," I said, as I paid him his share of the machine's proceeds. "I hope you're not working too hard."

"Thank you very much," he said. "On the contrary, I fear I am not working hard enough." He bowed slightly, excused himself, and returned to the back of the store, where he began opening cartons of soap. I looked toward Mary-Lou for explanation. For once she stopped giggling. She shook her head.

"He is running a big truck garden outside of town,"

she said, "and he is running the store, and it is not going well, any of it. It is very sad."

"I'm sorry to hear it," I said. I had replaced a half-full globe of gumballs with a full one, and I held the half-full one out to Mary-Lou.

"I like the orange ones best," Mary-Lou said, giggling once again as her slender hand came out of the globe holding five orange gumballs.

At three-forty-five I stopped for coffee—and to service a machine—in a dimly lighted old counter restaurant, almost a classic of its kind, with ancient gold-leaf signs painted on the windows announcing sodas, sundaes, and booths for ladies. Near the cash register there was a glass cabinet full of penny candy and a rack of fatigued magazines. A small stand covered with dusty drug items stood near the door, and the counter back-bar was dotted with fancy printed signs bearing such legends as "No checks cashed. We know your check is okay—it's the bank we don't trust." There were a few hand-lettered placards, too, proclaiming, "All pies baked on premises," and "coffee 10, refill 5." It was a Momma-Poppa store, run by Momma and Poppa Johanssen, and it was so dark you could never tell without going in whether it was open or closed.

As I sat down at the counter, Mr. Johanssen appeared in the doorway to the kitchen. He was tall, skinny, gray, and slightly bent. He seemed to wear a perpetual look of resignation.

"Oh, it's you," he said.

"I'd like a cup of coffee, please," I said.

Mr. Johanssen nodded up and down slowly.

"Why not?" he said. "That's all we ever sell—dime cups of coffee."

"Now that's not true, Elva!" Momma Johanssen's voice came out of the kitchen. She appeared in the doorway, a big, husky, graying woman obviously made for motherhood and cooking. She looked at me. "He done real good yesterday!" she said. She turned back to her husband. "And you know it! Seventeen dinners—fourteen specials and three à la carte. And scads of coffee!"

"Sounds good to me," I said.

Mr. Johanssen set a cup of coffee down in front of me.

"I suppose you want cream," he said.

"No, thanks. Black is fine."

Johanssen turned to his wife. "Seventeen dinners?" he said. "We should be selling *seventy!*"

"I don't know if I could cook seventy dinners, dear," said Mrs. Johanssen.

"You used to cook for the threshing crew, didn't you?" Poppa asked.

"The threshing crew ate what they got," Momma said. "But this here's a restaurant."

Mr. Johanssen turned back to me. "It's the location that's against us," he said resignedly. "There's no parking, no nothing except a few coffee customers. Mostly like that fat butcher down the street, too. You ask him does he want a refill, and he says, 'Just gimme enough to cover the bottom of the cup,' or maybe 'Just a splash, please,' and then he don't expect to pay nothing for it. Him and the barber, and a couple of them old pensioners from the front rooms they rent out across the street. But," he said, nodding significantly, "I've got my eye on another place."

"Oh, Pa," said Mrs. Johanssen, shaking her head, "you know it ain't no better than this one. Or the last one."

"That's what you say, Myra," Poppa said. "That's what you say. But I got my eye on it all the same. It's near a the-ayter, and that's what brings in the business, you know."

"The the-ayter's closed," Momma said.

"But it'll open again," Poppa said, "and when it does, we'll be in that new place, you watch and see!" The old man straightened up a little. "I've got some ideas I ain't let on about yet—about fixin' that place up. All it needs is paint, and you know how I handle a paintbrush. Why, that's a fine place. Why, when we get in there, you'll be cookin' seventy dinners, Myra, and God knows how many lunches, and maybe have a girl in to help you, and we'll be makin' lots of money!"

Poppa Johanssen's eyes were shining as he issued this proclamation. Momma looked at him wistfully for a moment, and then she smiled at him and wiped her hands on her apron.

"Maybe you're right at that, Elva," she said. "Could be it's the one we've been looking for."

Jotto Baker's delicatessen and liquor store was my first post-coffee stop. Jotto's name had once been Giotto Bouscarella, but since few people could pronounce it, and none spell it, he'd altered it slightly. Jotto loved faded blue fabrics—factory-faded, that is—and he wore faded blue denim pants, faded blue shirts, faded blue canvas shoes (with red rubber soles) and a faded blue yachtsman's cap.

"How's the family?" Jotto asked me. He remembered them from a couple of previous servicing trips when both Mary-Armour and Jamie had been along.

"They're fine, thanks," I said.

"Say, that boy of yours," Jotto said, "he like airplanes?"

Actually, Jamie didn't care much one way or the other, but I said sure, he was crazy about them. After all, you can never tell when somebody is going to come forth with a toy, and you don't want to be on record as having a kid who is anti-airplane.

"Tell you what I'll do," Jotto said breezily. "I'll fly low over your house some Sunday and let him get a good look at my crate. Where you live—Sonoma?"

"A few miles outside," I said. "Say, that would be really nice, Jotto. I'll draw you a map of where it is."

"Sure, I'll give the kid a treat," Jotto said. "I just traded my Cub in on a new Beechcraft, and I want to log some hours anyway."

It was four o'clock when I left the faded-blue aviator, and I was beginning to think about going home. Before I called it a day, however, I made five more whirlwind calls —on Louis, who ran a chili parlor and came from Denmark and had spent twenty years on sailing ships; on Harry, the genial Scot in Mr. Fortalezza's market, who presided over the sale of delicious home-made pizzas; on George, the sleepy-eyed short-order cook from Des Moines, who had put 4,784 beans into an irregularly shaped jar and asked his customers to guess how many, and who didn't suspect foul play (I did) when one customer, the husband of one of George's waitresses, guessed the number right on the nose; on Mr. Leath, the friendly Texan who ran a tiny store on the edge of town when he could take time from his fishing; and finally on Mr. Pulnawski, who was Polish, and whose children annoyed him by failing to believe his harrowing stories about the rigors of his Minnesota childhood.

Then, nearly exhausted, but with a good load of pennies, I drove home.

The sight of a wife and child playing on a green lawn under the watchful eye of a large bounding dog is a healing thing indeed.

"How'd it go?" Mary-Armour asked, as I unwound myself from the car and wound myself around her. It was awfully handy having a Board Chairman you liked to kiss.

"We're doing better," I said. "I figure we'll run ten per cent ahead of last month—if it keeps up, that is. I've still got two more days of collecting."

"It'll keep up," Mary-Armour said.

Her confidence was reassuring, and for a moment I tried to forget that what we needed, if we were ever going to reach Chugwater's fabled $100-a-week net, was not a 10 per cent increase in sales, but a 310 per cent one.

10

That night I had a nightmare, an awful one. I went through everything—cold sweat, hot sweat, the inability to talk, run, or fight back. Naturally, I would like to be able to tell you that my nightmare stemmed from some heroic war experience, but the plain facts are that it was scripted by Henry Skill.

The night had started out badly with me awake, brooding over the fact that our best monthly gross to date—ignoring the month now being collected—was $415.97. With a little mental arithmetic I soon came up with the astonishing statistic that, at this rate, someone was dropping seven-eighths of a penny into one of our machines every minute of the day and night (or seven pennies every eight minutes, if you're offended, as I am, by the thought of someone using a clipped coin).

Staring at the black ceiling, I turned this figure over in my mind, and after awhile I began to wonder whether at that particular moment someone was putting a penny in a machine. Anxiously I started running through the list of locations in my mind, ticking off those stores that were sure to be closed and where, therefore, the machines were incommunicado. At last I narrowed the chase to a small handful of late-closing hash-houses, bar-grocery combinations, and drive-ins.

I suppose it was at about this point I dropped off to sleep, because I remember the next scene too vividly for any real-life happening. A car, a model-A roadster, pulled up to the drive-in, and a group of nice-looking high-school students got out and came into the building. They grouped themselves informally around the jukebox—my bulk vender stood right next to it—and while the jukebox played "Penny Serenade," they dropped coins into my machine and chomped up large quantities of gum. Some of them blew enormous bubbles.

And then, almost before I knew it, three twin-piped V-8s full of ducktail haircuts roared up to the drive-in. The drive-in doors burst open as the group swarmed inside, an ugly bunch obviously hopped up with booze and dope. My attractive teen-agers scattered as the newly-arrived juvenile delinquents took over. The jukebox music was now coming in big lurching sobs, as though the turntable were off center; the lights flickered oddly; everyone was chartreuse or violet. Laughing insanely, the pachucos began to rock my machine back and forth, back and forth; the music stumbled, auto horns blew; the vandals cackled, "Reet, reet!" and someone shouted my name. The machine rocked left, then right, hovered delicately on the balance point, and then agonizingly went all the way over. I clawed the air frantically while the glass smashed into a million tinkling slivers, and the silver, pink, vermilion, mauve, and ochre gumballs spattered over acres of checkered linoleum like fissioning particles from an atomic explosion.

The next thing I knew, Mary-Armour was gripping my pajama top and saying in a sympathetic voice, "You're all right, you're all right."

I sat bolt upright. "My God!" I said, wiping a cold hand across my moist forehead. "They . . . they . . ." I was about to say they had destroyed my machine, but by this time I was beginning to move back into the real world. I drew in a deep breath and let it go out slowly.

"There," Mary-Armour said. "It was just a dream."

"I think I'm suffering from a guilt complex," I said.

"Guilt? What about?"

"The route," I said.

"Why should you feel guilty about the route?"

"Nobody trusts me," I said.

"Of course they trust you."

"No," I said, "even my most friendly locations don't really think our machines give out a penny's worth for a penny. Even if it belches out a pound of merchandise, they still think it's some sort of cheat. I've even started to believe it myself."

"That's silly," Mary-Armour said reprovingly.

"You know that hundred-count gum?"

"The big ones?"

"That's right, the big ones. That's a heck of a lot of bubble gum for a penny. But do you know what a kid said to me today? He said it was a gyp because they were hollow."

"Well, that's ridiculous. Don't you even think about it."

"They suspect me," I said.

"Who suspects you?"

"Everyone. Grocers, kids, everyone. They think the metal charms never come out of the Boston Bean machines. They think they're glued to the glass."

"Well, they're not. We know that."

"Or else they think they're too big to come out through the vending slot."

"Well, some of them are," Mary-Armour said.

"I know it!" I said. "Can I help it if I made a buying error? Whose side are you on, anyway?"

"Take it easy, darling. I'm on your side."

"Well, I should think!" I said. I was breathing hard. "You know what that old bat who runs the Vista Café said to me today? I'd put on a new Boston Bean thing last time I was there. She said her kid put in ten pennies and all she got was beans. No charms. And do you know what she said—the old bat, I mean?"

"What did she say?"

"She looked at me—real sad, you know—and said, 'If you could only have seen her little face!'"

"Well, don't let that worry . . ."

"As though the sight of her kid's crummy little puss would make me want to give her all the charms in the globe, free, gratis! I'd like to *kick* that kid's face, that's what!"

"No, you wouldn't."

"Well, I'd like to kick the old bat, then!"

"No, you wouldn't."

"Well, I'd like to kick *someone!*"

"No, you wouldn't," Mary-Armour said. "All you want is to have the route run smoothly and make a little money. You don't want to kick anyone, and you know it. Now, why don't you try to go back to sleep."

"Then there was this grocer last week—told me I was ruining kids' teeth. You know—sugar in the gum."

"He didn't handle sugar himself?"

"I don't know. Maybe not."

"Did he sell soft drinks?"

"I don't know."

"Well, he must sell canned fruit, doesn't he? Canned fruit's loaded with sugar!"

"Yeah?"

"Of course. He's just as bad as you are."

"I don't like the way you said that," I said.

"Oh, for goodness sakes, unwind, will you?" Mary-Armour said.

I took a deep breath and thought about it.

"Go on," Mary-Armour said. "Lie down. Let's get some sleep."

"Okay," I said. "I guess you're right. I've got a big day ahead of me."

I lay my head back on the pillow, and Mary-Armour turned off her bedside light.

"You know that Mrs. Mather?" I said. "The one who runs that doughnut shop? She's been married forty-five years."

"That's nice." Mary-Armour's voice sounded drowsy.

"You know what she did when I came by last week? She said it was her anniversary. Took me into the back room and gave me a big slug of Old Taylor to help her celebrate."

"You told me. That was nice of her."

"She's a nice old lady."

"Most of your people are nice. Like that Freddie Wing Ding."

"Wing Duck," I said.

"All right, Wing Duck. Let's go to sleep."

I thought the whole thing over for a while. "Yeah, mostly they're okay," I said. I turned over on my side. "She gave me darn near half a tumblerful—old Mrs. Mather. Then she wanted me to have another, but I wouldn't."

"That doesn't sound like you."

I ignored that one.

"No, you're right," I said. "They're mostly very nice people. There's just a few like that buzzard Skill. That skinflint! I'd like to kick his—"

"*Go to sleep!*" Mary-Armour said.

After a while, I did.

I was on the road the next morning by eight o'clock. Oh, I tell you, I felt pretty perky. "There's nothing like a good, early start!" I kept telling myself. I even said it out loud once or twice as I neared the town of Napa, and in between times I whistled loudly enough to have been all Seven Dwarfs.

By eleven o'clock I was still in a fine frame of mind, having ticked off eleven locations and being just about to finish my twelfth. I was standing on the sidewalk amid a gently blowing mass of newspapers and old candy wrappers, servicing the tab-gum machine in front of Dale's Drugs & Sundries. I had my tall plywood gum-loader open, leaning against the stand that held the two machines. I was singing "Now you can roll a sil-ver dol-lar down up-paw-wun the ground, and it'll ro-ho-holl . . ."

Fatty Dale stuck his half-dozen chins out the swinging front door of his store.

"You sound pretty goddam happy," he said drily.

". . . be-cuz it's row-how-hound . . ." I said, nodding to him politely. "A wo-man nev-er knows what a good man she's got . . ."

And then it happened. A sudden gust of wind. It caught the gum-loader as though it were a sail. Over it went with a crash, face down, and 1,700 pieces of chewing gum in ten not-so-assorted flavors lay in a heap on the sidewalk.

Fatty Dale shrugged and cocked his head on one side. ". . . un-til she turns him dow-how-how-hown . . ." he sang, and then disappeared inside his drugstore.

For a moment I stood in silence, staring down at the mess. I wanted to hit something, shout a dirty word, or blame someone, possibly Fatty Dale. But there was nothing really suitable to hit, blame, or shout at, except myself. Gritting my teeth, I set the tall, empty gum carrier upright, knelt beside it, and began to restock it from the jumbled pile of gum.

Forty-five minutes later I was on the road once more, vowing that I would never, ever, under any circumstances, be so careless as to leave the loader open and unattended again.

Little by little, as I drove along, my spirits began to climb back to normal. It was really a beautiful day. I saw several crew-cut boys driving pastel convertibles with tops down, co-piloted by girls sitting in the middle of the front seats, their long straw-colored bobs blowing in the wind. Ah, spring, ah, youth, I thought.

A few minutes later I saw a sign that read CAUTION— VETERAN PEDESTRIANS. I slowed down, contemplating the wisdom of warning innocent drivers like myself about the lurking treacheries of wily, case-hardened old pedestrians. A minute later I passed the entrance to the hospital for war veterans. Then I entered Yountville.

At first I was surprised—every third car in Yountville that day seemed to be a taxicab. Usually it was every second car. In fact, I believe it is safe to generalize on the fact that Yountville, at any time of night or day, at all seasons of the year, has more cabs per capita than any other town in America. They're constantly in use, too, shuttling the veterans back and forth from the hospital to the numerous shoddy bars that line the highway.

The patients in the hospital, poor souls, are mainly World War I soldiers. Some even still wear bits of World War I garb—scoutmaster hats, for instance, the kind still worn (in the movies, at least) by Canadian mounties. Their existence, as seen from the road, is a deadly one. It starts with breakfast at the hospital, and then the cab ride to The Little Grass Shack for the day's first beer and the day's first anesthetic of small talk. And then along about noon—or afternoon, what the hell, it doesn't matter

—they ride back in a cab, or if it's a nice day (and it usually is), some of them walk back to the hospital. For many it's a slow, hobbling walk down the railroad track that parallels the road, but time doesn't matter, because there's too much of it already.

I got out of my car at a Yountville grocery and began to service a machine. An old veteran, his face a network of crimson veins, stopped to watch.

"Hello," I said. "How's it going?"

"Oh, I'll live," he said. "And if I don't, it's paid for."

He walked on into the store and came out a few minutes later with something cylindrical in a brown paper sack.

If the hospital weren't there, I thought, Yountville wouldn't be there, either. And yet Yountville had been there first. Somehow I thought of Petaluma; if the chickens hadn't been there, Petaluma would never have been there. Or would it? Which came first, the chicken or the Egg Basket of the World? My mind ran back briefly to my first visit to Petaluma. I remembered my amazement as I saw, in rapid succession, a tiny restaurant with a good-sized fishing vessel sitting on top of it, its bow and stern projecting over the front and rear roof-lines of the café; an ancient life-size automobile further down the street, mounted fifteen feet up in the air on top of a metal pole; a huge rectangular box the size of a freight car, rotating constantly atop a building in the middle of town, advertising See's Candies. What Freudian impulse, I wondered, drove Petalumians to put heavy things way up high where they didn't belong?

The two Yountville machines yielded $6.23, as against $5.38 the previous month.

Fifteen minutes later I pulled up in front of Angie Phelps' ice-cream parlor. I picked up my scale, my penny bag, my other equipment, and walked in. Angie was a large-boned man about thirty-five, filling out nicely under the effect of continuous exposure to his own ice creams and syrups. I found him leaning on his ice-cream cabinet, clad in dungarees and an undershirt, reading a comic book.

"Say, got your card," he said, as I set down my equipment. "Didn't know you was from New York."

Angie was referring to a mimeographed post card Mary-Armour and I had sent out to each location—real hotshot public relations—telling them who we were, and wishing everyone good luck.

"Yep," I said. "Little old Manhattan."

"I used to live in the East myself," Angie said. "Minneapolis. Have an aunt lives in Syracuse, New York, too. You wouldn't know nobody from Syracuse, New York, would you?"

"Angie," I said, "Syracuse is a long way from New York City."

"I just thought I'd ask," Angie said.

"How long ago did you come out here?" I asked, as I opened the bulk machine and removed the coin box.

"Five years."

"Been back to Minneapolis since?"

"Only once. And buh-rother, you can have it!"

"Sold on California, eh?"

"Yeah," Angie said. He took a comb from his back pocket and began to comb his brown hair, pressing a few large waves in with the heel of his hand. "Mostly. Only I miss all them different seasons we used to have back East."

"You mean like winter?" I said. "And spring and fall?"

"Those are the ones," Angie said.

"Angie," I said, scoring up $4.23 on my route card, "the seasons change out here."

"Sure," Angie said, putting the comb in his back trouser pocket. "It rains and it don't rain. Two seasons."

"No, Angie, what I mean is that you just have to *look*

to see them change. Saying that California doesn't have a change of seasons is just as unrealistic as saying that New York City is a nice place to visit, but no place to live."

"How much did you take out of there?" Angie asked.

"Four twenty-three, Angie," I said. "What you have to realize is that just because it only snows once a century in this valley, it doesn't mean that we don't have winter. Why, winter in the Napa Valley is a season just as definite as twelve below zero in Minneapolis."

"Yeah," Angie said. "What commission do I get, anyhow? I forget."

"You get twenty per cent on the bulk, fifteen per cent on the tab. That's standard."

"Only fifteen per cent on the tab? How come?"

"That merchandise costs me more, Angie. Listen, next winter you just take yourself a look around. You'll see a lot of trees and shrubs dropping their leaves, just the way they do back East. And you know how the quail and ducks and everything migrate right through here, don't you? Sure you do. And all the animals grow winter coats —even your old tomcat there grows one. Maybe it's not as thick as the one he'd grow if he lived in Minneapolis, but it's a winter coat all the same."

"That cat's seven years old," Angie said, cocking his head on one side. "Would you believe it?"

"The hills turn brown when winter comes," I said, "and the rain rains, and winds blow, and roofs leak—it's just like any place else, only the changes are more subtle."

Angie nodded up and down as he wiped the top of the ice-cream cabinet with a greasy dishtowel.

"Even a newcomer like me can tell that winter's here without having to shovel two feet of snow off the walk," I said.

Angie kept on nodding. I added up the total commissions from the two machines and paid him. Then for a moment we both stood silent, looking out the front window at the brilliant sunshine.

"Wonderful day, isn't it?" I said.

Angie nodded up and down in silent agreement. Finally he sighed. "But I sure do miss the change of seasons," he said.

At Thelma's Sweet Shoppe, which was my next stop, a beautiful sight greeted me. The tab-gum machine glistened as though I had just shined it. I wondered if Frank Hoppe, the grizzled old gnome who ran Thelma's, had wiped it off by mistake; for it's an unwritten law of gumballing that no matter how spotless the storekeeper may keep the rest of his store, he will not wipe one speck of dust from the gum machine.

The most beautiful part of what I saw, though, was not the gleaming, unscratched machine—it was the fact that in one week, it had emptied completely.

"Frank, we're in business!" I said.

Frank assembled his wrinkled features into a smile.

"Yeah, it did okay this week, didn't it?" he agreed.

"Can't do any better than that," I said. I opened the machine, leaned the tall gum-carrier against it and opened it, too. Then I began to reload the machine.

"I want to see how you do that," Frank said. As he came around the end of his candy counter, his hip accidentally brushed the top of the gum-carrier.

"Oops," he said.

But it was too late. The gum carrier had leaned past the perpendicular, and even though I caught it, the tall stacks of gum cascaded onto the tile floor.

"Say, I'm sure sorry!" Frank said.

I held my breath and counted to twenty-five.

"That's okay, Frank," I said.

"Well, guess I better get to work," Frank said. "Got to make up a batch of peanut brittle."

"Sure, Frank," I said. "You get to work."

As I started to pick up the gum, three small boys gathered around to watch. Observation was one phenomenon to which I was well accustomed. After a few minutes of silence, the middle-sized boy spoke.

"Need some help?"

"Thanks," I said. "I better do it myself—it all has to be sorted. What's your name?"

"Donny."

"What's his name?" I stopped picking up gum and motioned with my head toward the larger boy.

"His name's Joey," the middle-sized boy said.

I looked at the smallest boy.

"I'm Roy Rogers," he said.

"Yeah?" I said. "Have some gum." I gave them each a stick of Doublemint, which was a slow seller anyway, and tended to go stale.

"Gee, thanks!"

"Thanks."

"Thanks, mister."

Three for three—I almost fell over backwards in astonishment.

"Do you do this for a living?" the middle-sized boy asked.

"I suppose you might put it that way," I said.

"Gee!" Roy Rogers chimed in, his eyes popping, "that must be the bestest job in the world!"

I snorted with pleasure and gave them each a handful of nice, fresh Juicy Fruit.

Before starting the afternoon rounds, I buttressed myself with a sandwich, a can of beer, and a prune orchard. This turned out to be a wise precaution, inasmuch as the ball-gum vender at my next stop up the valley road, Barkis Jordan's Washington Market, was completely and uncontestably jammed.

"Damn thing's been stuck for over two weeks!" Jordan

complained peevishly. "Don't you ever come around any more?"

Even with my small experience, I was able to identify the Gum-Jam Syndrome right off: patient displays slight puffiness under the eyes, complains of a persistent craving to drink gum operator's blood; cannot rid self of sensation that gum machine, which jammed the night before last, has been out of order for a couple of months.

"I'm sorry it jammed up on you, Mr. Jordan," I said. I consulted my route cards. "Let's see, I was here exactly one week ago today. It was working then."

"Like hell it was!" Jordan snapped. "It's been out two, three weeks! There's been a million kids wanting gum— I must of lost at least five bucks worth of business on account of that damn thing!"

"I'll get it fixed right away," I said.

"Far as I'm concerned, you can take it with you," Jordan said angrily. "I'm fed up with it jamming night and day!"

A customer diverted Jordan's attention briefly by plunking a load of groceries down on his checkout counter. Jordan's tongue dripped honey, talking to the customer, while I opened the machine and began to work at the jam with my ice-pick. I hoped that by the time I had it fixed, Jordan might have cooled off.

As usual, I found that some crafty gum addict had dropped something unconstitutional down the penny slot. In this case, it looked like play money. Play money, I had discovered already, was the number-one jamming agent used in near-school areas. I would gladly have committed arson if I could only have found the factory where it was made.

But at that, play money was no worse than the insulation slugs, buttons, groschen und pfennigs, hacksaw blades, cigarette butts, cardboard, yen, and other bizarre objects I had removed from gum machines in the recent past. And in a way, I knew I should be thankful that it wasn't a chewing-gum jam; a chewing-gum jam occurs when some zealot with lots of energy and a certain amount of skill forces an entire mouthful of gum through the coin slot, thereby immobilizing the machine completely and turning the gum operator prematurely gray.

I took the coin mechanism apart, shook out a small aluminum disc stamped "25," and reassembled the mechanism. Then, while Mr. Jordan took care of a small line-up of customers, I weighed out the money and went through the polishing routine. Finally, when Jordan had finished short-changing his last customer, I paid him his $1.27.

"Okay," he growled, "now take it out."

"Why, it's all fixed now, Mr. Jordan," I said. "It had this piece of play money jamming it. Probably won't jam again for a year."

"It'll jam the minute you're out of the store," he said. "It always does."

"Mr. Jordan," I said. "I've kept records on this machine. This is the first time—"

"Listen, brother," Jordan cut in, "I'm trying to run a grocery store, see. I got work to do. So what happens? I'm working in the back of the store. A kid comes in. He puts a penny in the machine, and nothing comes out. So he comes to me—'I put a penny in that machine,' he says 'and nothing come out.' So what do I do? I leave whatever I'm doing and come to the front of the store and make sure he's turned the goddam handle. And if the machine ain't working, I've got to give the little so-and-so his money back—for all I know, his mother may be one of my customers!"

"Well, I'll gladly refund any pennies you've had to give out," I said. "That's a standing offer."

"You heard me," he said. "Out!" He spat on the floor and glared at me. Then he turned and walked to the back of his store.

A number of uncharitable thoughts about Mr. Jordan crossed my mind as I detached the machine from its bracket and detached the bracket from the wall. I finally deposited machine and bracket in the back seat of the station wagon and climbed in behind the wheel.

That ape, I told myself! By golly, he won't make me miss a single day's income! I'll relocate that machine this very minute—and in a far better spot than Barkis Jordan's crummy market!

I turned around in my seat, reloaded the machine with a fresh globe of 100-count, and climbed back out of the Jeep. I walked down the street till I came to a meat market I'd had my eye on for some time. I pushed open the door and walked in. Even before I had a chance to open my mouth, I heard a voice rasp at me from the back of the store.

"The answer is *no!*" the voice said.

I then saw the portly figure of a straw-hatted butcher peering at me belligerently from the door of a walk-in refrigerator. Had it not been for the cost of bubble gum, and a new glass globe, and the expense of replacing bent and broken parts, I would have brained him on the spot with my machine.

I made two more tries after that—one in a restaurant, and one in a bakery—but it was no go. It was the same old story. Most merchants I called on, unless they'd just been minted, had been propositioned by gumball operators for several decades, the penny-gum machine being something less than a fresh idea. They had already had their share of sad experiences with operators who gave them bad service, or no service, or cheated on the commission. Therefore, when I tried to enrich their lives with one of my gum machines, they looked at me, at my machine, and listened to my percentage. If any one of the three was a mite below par, my cause was lost.

I decided to try one more location, and then the hell with it, I'd throw the machine in the nearest river. The spot I picked didn't look profitable, but it looked easy. It was called Jepson's Market. Jepson's already had six assorted penny machines in front of the store, two to a stand, and I figured that the proprietor probably had some sort of fetish about them. And if he did, he could hardly turn down the deal I was going to propose.

"Mr. Jepson," I said to the tall, thin, gray-haired man who stood at the vegetable counter, arranging a display of avocados, "my name is Nelson."

"Hanks is the name," he said. "Jepson died ten, eleven years ago. Say," he said, brightening, "what you got there?"

"It's a new kind of penny machine," I said.

"That so?" he said eagerly. "What does it do?"

Enthusiasm was a reaction I was ill-prepared to meet.

"Well, it . . . it vends gumballs," I said, "and . . . well, all sorts of things."

"Looks like a dandy!" he said. "What's the deal?"

I still get a feeling of shame when I think about it, but I offered Mr. Hanks a commission of only five per cent. He accepted it as gratefully as though I'd given him the machine, gratis, along with a lifetime supply of bubble gum.

When I started the Jeep up once more, my guilt lost itself in a feeling of elation. Of course, I knew that Jepson's wasn't much of a location. Mr. Hanks had merely added my machine to the string of old, battered penny-catchers that, for some reason known only to those store-keepers who do it, he hauled in and out of his store once each day. (I thought ruefully of Og's words that my machines would "knock the competition right out" of any place worth having.) For the next month or so, I knew that my machine would do the lion's share of the penny business, because its newness would draw all the trade. But after that the business would settle down into an age-old pattern in which the venders present would split up the penny melon almost equally, the addition of my machine meaning only that each operator got a slightly smaller slice. And I can tell you with authority, incidentally, that there is no sight quite so agonizing as that of a small boy casing seven penny machines, one of which (the clean, well-shined one on the left) is yours, and finally putting his coin in the oldest, grubbiest klunk of the lot.

Such a thought, however, could not punch a hole in my joy at having got a location. I decided a celebration was in order. So I sidetracked two miles off the main road and dropped in on the Montreux winery.

I had made my first call on M. Montreux several months before, because I had heard that his red wine was the best in the area (in our price range, anyway). I made subsequent calls partly because this was true, partly because M. Montreux *looked* so French (beret, neckerchief, gray mustache, seamy French face), and partly because it was pleasant to talk to him about wine, about farming, about the days when he was big in the liquor business and traveled the United States extensively, about the decline of letter-writing, about his native France, or about the fact that the moon, when viewed from his front porch, was larger than when viewed from any other spot in the county.

M. Montreux's winery was only one of many I had visited in the course of my gumball duties, but had his wine been pure vinegar, I think I would have kept going back for more. For where else, I ask you, could I have found a congenial vintner who also raised sheep and who, during lambing time, would take an itinerant gumball merchant on a conducted tour of his flocks, pointing out the woolly new additions of a few days ago, the stillbulgy ewes nearly ready to drop their young, and behind a shed that housed a pump, a wobbly wet lamb not yet two hours old standing awkwardly beside its mother. Besides, M. Montreux's wine was very good and did not resemble vinegar in any way.

Unfortunately for me, M. Montreux was in San Francisco on business. From his foreman I purchased a gallon of red wine for $1.25, and headed back to the gum route.

My elation carried over to Harvey's Superette, where it was reinforced by finding both machines completely empty. The combined coin boxes contained $15.04. Mr. George Harvey, who got $3.01 of this, was most cordial.

The next two stops were the same. Unprecedented amounts of money in the coin boxes, and nothing but smiles on the faces of the storekeepers. This was more like it—my luck seemed to have changed. My only fear was that this good fortune might presage a disaster far greater than anything that had gone before.

But no disaster materialized. The day finished beautifully. I figured we were now running 20 per cent ahead of the previous month. At home that night, while Mary-Armour spooned cereal into Jamie, I poured M. Montreux's burgundy into five green unlabeled bottles, and corked four of them. With the fifth bottle I filled two wine glasses, and handed one to Mary-Armour.

"Here's to the upturn in business," I said.

We clinked our glasses together and sipped the wine.

"It does look good, doesn't it?" Mary-Armour said.

"The wine or the route?" I said.

"Both," Mary-Armour said. She set her glass down and shoveled some more food into Jamie. "Incidentally, the paper boy wants a deck of cards."

"I beg your pardon?"

"The paper boy," Mary-Armour said. "He wants a deck of cards."

"Well, it's a changing world," I said. "In my day, paper

boys saved up for new bikes, or maybe to buy a model-A Ford, if they were old enough to drive. But now they want playing cards. Well . . ." I shrugged. *"The Paper Boy with the Golden Arm.* Make someone a nice little book title."

"He wants some of those *little, teeny* playing cards, darling," Mary-Armour said. "The kind we put in with Boston Beans as charms."

"Oh, *those,*" I said. "Well, thank goodness. Sure, go ahead and give him some."

"We're all out."

"Then I'll get some more," I said. "Thank God! I thought the moral fiber of Sonoma County's youth was disintegrating!"

Mary-Armour took a sip of her wine and looked at me coolly over the top of her glass.

"You knew what I meant all the time, didn't you?" she said. "Honestly, I don't know why I don't grind you up and feed you to Cleo."

I slept well that night. No dreams, no nightmares. Just good solid sleep.

My charmed commercial life continued the next day. It was a long day, and even though collections sagged slightly, so that we were running only 15 per cent ahead instead of 20 per cent, I couldn't be too upset. After all, every location owner seemed unusually cheery and nice. And there were no jammed machines, no distraught butchers, no broken globes. In fact, the day's only problem came from one grocer having sprayed a machine liberally with a hose while washing his front windows.

As I drove homeward that night, having now collected from every machine on the route, I began wondering if maybe our public-relations post card could have anything to do with this rash of good feeling. In my head I began to sketch out the copy for post card number two.

Halfway down Highway 12 from Santa Rosa, I suddenly signaled a stop, threw on the brakes, and pulled off to the side of the road. There were two fine long pieces of two-by-six lumber lying just off the pavement. And while one of my least favorite sights was that of a big eighteen-wheel lumber truck bearing down on me, I still was quite willing to pick up anything the trucks dropped in transit.

I opened the back of the station wagon and thrust the two boards inside. I removed the red hunting cap I had begun to wear on my servicing rounds as a sort of trademark—almost no one could remember my name or face, but they could remember the hat—and thumbtacked it to the protruding ends of the lumber as a sort of flag. I was whistling as I climbed back into the car; these two planks would not only finish the doghouse I was building for Cleo, but they would also nearly put me even with Mary-Armour, who on her way home from the grocery a week before, had picked up three nine-foot-long two-by-fours.

I kept on whistling, thinking of the tableau that awaited me at home—wife and child dallying on the greensward under the eyes of our faithful new dog.

They were all in front of the house, all right, when I arrived home, but the total effect was not quite what I'd expected. Jamie and Cleo were sitting side by side on the porch steps, both quiet for a change, and Mary-Armour was standing in the drive. Beside her stood Mr. Simmons, our prune-growing neighbor, ears akimbo supporting his eternal straw hat, his mouth looking like a trap that had snapped shut.

"Why, hello there, Mr. Simmons," I said heartily as I got out of the car. "Nice to see you."

"You won't think it's so all-fired nice," the old man said belligerently, "when you learn why I'm here!"

"Cleo came home with one of Mr. Simmons' chickens in her mouth," Mary-Armour explained soberly. "About half an hour ago."

"Cleo?" I said in amazement. "Why, Cleo's hardly big enough—"

"Oh, yes she is big enough!" Simmons broke in emphatically. "I saw her take it, too! Gettin' so a chicken ain't safe around here no more. And God knows how many *rabbits* she's ate!"

For a moment I considered saying that anyone who kept his rabbits the way Simmons did, deserved to have them eaten. I had been over to his place once, returning an exceedingly tame black-and-white rabbit that had wandered onto our front lawn, and had been amazed to see that less than half of the large number of rabbits he kept were in hutches. The remainder—a good thirty or forty rabbits—were scattered around the place—most of them at the time grouped around a large bale of hay near Simmons' woodshed, others peering out from beneath Simmons' house, and three or four nestled together comfortably in a swing on the front porch.

Simmons' chickens, however, were not granted the same liberties. Instead, they were confined to a flimsy chicken-wire pen adjacent to an ancient and crumbling hen-house. And since the subject of present discussion was the loss of one chicken, I swallowed my comments on the rabbit situation.

"I'm terribly sorry about your chicken," I began. "I . . ."

"I'd a' shot that dog if I'd a' had my gun!" Simmons said.

I turned and looked at the silent pair, dog and boy, sitting side by side on the front steps. They knew that something dramatic was going on.

"And I'd have had a perfect right to!" Simmons added angrily, sticking his face up close to mine.

"Well, I just couldn't be sorrier," I said. I shook my head helplessly. "I didn't have any idea Cleo was big enough . . ."

I really couldn't think of very much to say. Being a city boy, I didn't know what the etiquette of the situation demanded. I knew there was a pretty stern code regarding dogs that killed any kind of stock, but I wasn't too clear on the particulars. Maybe I was expected to march tight-lipped into the house, get a gun, and shoot the dog. Or perhaps shoot myself—I wasn't exactly sure which Simmons wanted.

"Naturally, I'll be glad to pay for the dead chicken," I said huskily.

"Hell, it didn't kill the chicken!" Simmons said. "Chicken's good as ever, damn her hide. She's flew up in your oak tree!"

I followed his gaze upward and saw a small Rhode Island Red, clucking contentedly from a high branch.

"Will she come down?" I said.

"Not for me, she won't," Simmons snapped. "Ain't my problem anyhow. Your dog got her up there—you get her down!"

"Well, of course," I said blandly. "I'll be glad to." I cleared my throat. "Here, chick, chick, chick," I said. "Chick, chick, chick."

"She seems to like it up there," Mary-Armour said. I gave her what I hoped was a withering look.

"He-e-e-e-re, chickie, chickie, chickie," I called. "Here, chick, chick, chick, chick, chick!"

"Chick, chick-a-boom, chick," Mary-Armour said.

"That's *not* helping," I said coldly.

"You got a ladder?" Simmons asked.

"Well, yes," I said. "But see how those bees are going in and out of that hole in the branch there? She's sitting right over the entrance to a big beehive. I sort of hate to disturb them."

Simmons shrugged. "Up to you," he said. "Any way you want to get her down."

"Here, chick, chick," I called. For all the good my

calling did, the chicken could have been made of china. Suddenly I got a brilliant idea. I turned to Simmons. "How'd you like to sell that chicken?" I said.

"Her?" Simmons said. He paused a minute and wiped his jaw with the palm of his hand before answering. "Why, she's one of my best chickens!"

I knew she would be.

"You would sell her, though, wouldn't you?" I asked.

Simmons took off his straw hat and rotated it on one finger.

"I'd sure hate to sell that one," he said. "She's a prize-winner, that chicken."

"What do chickens sell for?" I asked. "Forty, fifty cents a pound? Say fifty cents." I looked up at the stolid chicken. "She's about what—three or four pounds?"

"Four pounds?" Simmons said incredulously. "Why, man, you're standing a long ways away from that chicken! You get up close and take a look. If that chicken don't dress out at six pounds, I'll climb up there and get her myself!"

"I'll give you three dollars for her," I said.

"For a prize hen like that?"

"Three dollars," I said. "Or else we wait here for her to come down by herself."

"Well . . ." Simmons pulled his lips together and put his hat back on. "All right." He snuffled indignantly. "It's outrageous, but . . . all right."

I reached for my wallet and suddenly remembered that I had no bills. I had used my last paper dollar to pay a commission at my last stop. I looked at Mary-Armour and raised my eyebrows.

"You have some money, don't you?" I asked. She shook her head.

"Mr. Simmons," I said, "would you mind if I didn't pay you till tomorrow? I'll bring it by your house."

Simmons frowned. "Fine thing," he said. "First your

dog carries off one of my best chickens. Then you beat me down on the price. Now you want to *owe* me the money!"

Then I got my second brilliant idea.

"Come to think of it," I said, "I can pay you now, after all."

I got my penny scale, set it up on the hood of the Jeep, and weighed out three dollars. I poured it into the paper sack that had housed my sandwiches, and handed it to Simmons.

"What's this?" he said.

"Three dollars," I said.

He glared at the contents of the sack, and at me. Then, without a word, he walked down our driveway to the road.

The chicken stayed in the tree until dark, at which time we gave up our vigil. The following morning, Friday, Jamie and I rushed out to look for her. But she was gone.

We went back in the house and had breakfast, after which I started weighing and bagging the pennies collected during the preceding three days. I used our baby scales for this purpose, balance-type scales being generally more accurate than those that depend on stretching or compressing a spring. I weighed everything out into batches of fifty dollars, and when I finished, I had eight sacks—$400—and about fifteen dollars left over. Actually, I had collected $473.24, but quite a bit of it had been returned to merchants who wanted their commissions in the form of pennies. I tied the sacks shut with rope—seven of them, that is; I didn't have enough rope to tie the eighth—and I carried them out to the station wagon and got ready to drive to the bank.

"I'm on my way," I shouted into the house. Mary-Armour appeared at the door.

"Aren't you going to take the lawn mower to be sharpened?" she asked.

I sighed. "I guess so."

I walked toward the pumphouse to get the mower. As I entered the door, I saw a flash of color behind the pump. I peered around, and found our hen sitting there, looking up at me indignantly. I reached down and moved her aside. There, in a nest of old laundry rope, was a small, brown egg.

I picked it up and took it to Mary-Armour. "While I'm gone," I said, "try to decide whether you want future omelets or immediate fricassee."

Halfway to the bank a gray cat ran across the road in front of me. I jammed the brake pedal to the floor and heard the one untied sack of pennies roll forward, showering the floor of the front seat with copper. I pulled off the road, got out the left-hand door, and came around to the right-hand side of the car to do my clean-up. When I opened the right-hand door, a coppery Niagara sprayed out onto the road shoulder.

While I picked the pennies up, I tried to divert my mind by figuring out how soon, at our present rate of increase, we would be making $100 a week. If we just continued to better our sales by 15 per cent each month, it would mean that the next month we would gross . . . let's see, $544? or $644? I stopped picking up the pennies and got out a piece of paper. Let's see, it would be $544 gross next month, $625 the next, $719 the next. The month after that we would gross $927, and the month after that, $1,066. Forty per cent of $1,066 was $426.40; we would have that much left after we had paid commissions and merchandise costs.

Of course, we would still have to pay gas and oil out of that, and depreciation and taxes and licenses and all the rest, but I was willing to forget that for the moment. I didn't want anything to spoil the realization that if we just kept on increasing our take at the current rate for five more months, we would actually have Og Chugwater's $100-a-week!

I suddenly felt good inside. I didn't mind picking up the pennies at all.

I parked in front of the bank and walked in, carrying a sack of pennies in each hand. I dropped them noisily on the floor under one of the stand-up desks by the wall and went back out to the Jeep for two more sacks. And then for two more, and two more after that.

I noticed several depositors watching me out of the sides of their eyes. With a studied indifference to everyone, I made out my deposit slip and approached the teller's window. Only the teller and I knew what was in those sacks. As far as the other customers were concerned, the bags might contain quarters, or halves, or maybe even silver dollars.

And maybe I was a wealthy oil baron.

11

Suddenly spring was almost gone, and summer was just around the corner. In the penny-gum business, summer means vacation—not vacation for the operator, but for the small fry who have been hanging around the school store drawing chalk pictures on the sidewalk and chewing bubble gum. Since almost all our best locations were near schools, Mary-Armour and I foresaw—until our small customers were called together once again by the school bell, that is—three months of reduced sales. This prospect did not appeal to executives planning a steady monthly sales increase.

The steel-trap mind of Multivend's president, however, was equal to this challenge.

"I've got the perfect solution," I told Mary-Armour after supper one night. Jamie was already in bed, and the two of us were sitting across from one another at the kitchen table, both eager to stall off the moment when we'd have to get up and wash dishes.

"Solution to what?" Mary-Armour asked.

"To what we were just talking about: school vacations."

"Oh. What are we going to do?"

"We're going to buy half a dozen used machines at fifteen dollars apiece, and I'm going to take them up to the Russian River."

"And throw them in? Why only six?"

"Sweetie . . ." I said, as ominously as possible.

"Well, that's what you're always threatening to do," she said.

"Listen, be serious," I said. And then I explained what she already knew, but listened to again anyway because it was easier than washing dishes. I told her how a large part of the Redwood Empire, as our local newspaper called it, was just now getting ready for a big tourist influx. Most of the establishments in the Russian River area, I said, counted on making more in the three summer months than they made all the rest of the year. In fact, a lot of these places opened only for the summer. Six gum machines, strategically placed by Multivend's skilled locating staff, namely me, would make up for a smaller take at our school locations.

"So you want to buy six more machines?"

"Kee-rect."

"At fifteen dollars apiece. Let's see. Six times fifteen— that's ninety dollars?"

"Kee-rect."

"Where are you going to get it?"

"The ninety bucks? Why, we've got ninety bucks, sweetie."

"I know we have. But if you spend it on machines, what are we going to pay our grocery bill with?"

"We're not quite that bad off yet," I said.

"But we're going to be—p.d.q.—if we keep on handing out our capital. Listen, we both know it's going to be a long pull with the machines—and that's okay—you can't just build a successful business overnight. But meanwhile, we're going to wind up picking grapes unless we watch our —if you'll pardon the expression—*pennies.*"

"All I'm trying to do," I said patiently, "is to keep our income from falling off this summer, so we won't have to dip into our capital even more."

"I know," Mary-Armour said, "but why not do it this way? We've got a lot of two-machine locations near schools, haven't we? Sure we have. At least six of them. They won't bring in much this summer. So why not take one machine from each of these locations and put *them* up on the Russian River? And leave the other machine at the school store, just to . . . well, sort of hold the franchise."

"Sweetie-pie," I said, "you are a financial genius. How about letting me do the housework while you go out and put this route on a paying basis?"

Unfortunately, I was not able to shed my responsibilities that easily. Therefore, three days later, I found myself at the wheel of the Jeep, hauling six red gum machines toward the Russian River.

I attacked the Guerneville area of the river first, because it seemed to have a tremendous concentration of bars, motels, resorts, groceries, restaurants, and other points of human congregation. My quest, which took all day, was somewhat discouraging, because almost everyone was too busy to talk. They were all bustling about, taking down shutters, repainting, and getting ready for the horde they expected to pour in over Memorial Day week end.

I kept on buzzing around like a persistent fly, however, and by five o'clock I had rounded up what looked like three dandy two-machine locations. One was in River Vista, a resort large enough to be a town all by itself, another in a somewhat fancier establishment called the Essex

Inn, and the third in an arcade on the main street of Guerneville.

Memorial Day dawned cool and hazy, and the Russian River got off to a slow vacation start. It picked up very quickly, however, and our six machines began to do phenomenally well.

The weekly trips I made to the area added about forty miles to my rounds. I didn't mind the added mileage, though, because it was no chore to travel through the handsome country that surrounded the river. In fact, I looked forward to that part of the journey each week. I always counted on stopping long enough to pick a gallon of blueberries at the county's only blueberry farm, and I wouldn't have missed the raspberry sherbet cones at River Vista for anything. I always had two, both doubles, and while I was consuming them I would sit down in River Vista's paved outdoors and set myself up as a detached spectator of the passing parade. Under my microscope I put thousands of specimens just up from San Francisco for their two-weeks-with-pay at the River, all slacked and shorted and haltered, having the time of their lives on the asphalt under the River Vista redwoods. Being in a vacation spot, but not being on vacation myself, gave me a terribly smug, superior feeling. God knows why!

River Vista was owned by a pair of plump, fortyish twin brothers named Burkey, men of vision who had turned a pokey old redwood grove into a hard-surfaced paradise complete with snack bars, kiddie rides, cocktail lounges, a shooting gallery, and a thousand tiny cabins set a foot and a half apart. When these two entrepreneurs discovered how much business my two little machines were doing, they experienced an understandable change of heart about my presence. But since we had made a bargain, and since the machines didn't jam, and since the Burkeys were men of honor, they were reluctant to throw me out bodily.

"Say, fellow," Gene Burkey said to me one day near the end of June, after I'd taken better than fifteen dollars out of the two machines for the third week in a row, "you must have lots of better spots for your machines than this place." He smiled at me, the benevolent smile of a man who is not too busy to stop and help out a fellow creature. "Any time you want to move them, you just go right ahead."

"Thanks, Gene," I said, "but I'll stick it out with you guys."

A flutter of pain marred the benevolence of Burkey's smile.

"Main Street of Guerneville ought to do a big business," he said. "Ought to make this place look sick!"

"On the contrary," I said. "This place makes Guerneville look sick."

Burkey frowned and looked businesslike. "How about the Essex—you tried that?" he asked. "Lousy with people. Higher income group than this, too."

"I've got two machines there," I said.

Burkey folded his arms and looked away in irritation. Then he started on a new tack.

"Must be a lot out of your way to drive way up here each week," he said.

"A little," I said.

"How much?"

"About forty miles."

"Forty miles! Holy cow! Think of the gasoline! You're losing money, man!"

"No," I said. "Not actually."

"Well, you're losing time then. Time's money."

"I don't mind," I said. "It's a nice drive. Lovely country."

"Yeah. Lovely. Say, what percentage did you say we're getting on these things?"

"Fifteen per cent on the tab gum. Twenty on the bulk."

"Fifteen and twenty, eh? Hey, Joe . . ." His twin brother approached from the vicinity of the shooting gallery. "Joe, don't we get better than twenty per cent on the gum we sell over the counter?"

"Sure, Gene, we get about thirty."

There was silence, while they both looked at me accusingly. I smiled innocently.

"You fellows have certainly done a terrific job up here," I said.

More silence.

"This was just a lousy stretch of virgin forest until you guys got hold of it," I said. I smiled hopefully. "Looks like another good year for you, too!"

"Didn't you hear him?" Gene said to me. "We get thirty per cent on our own gum, and only fifteen per cent on yours."

"*Twenty* on the bulk," I corrected. "But listen, I don't compete with your sales, if that's what you're thinking about. Why, mine's all penny stuff—yours sells for a nickel a pack. All I do is round up the spare pennies that wouldn't get spent on your gum anyway."

"Listen," Gene said. "How about that drugstore in Guerneville. I bet that would be one terrific location! Why don't you take these machines and try 'em there?"

"Gentlemen," I said, "you're awfully decent to be willing to release me from our bargain. No kidding—I really appreciate it. But I'm like you—an agreement is an agreement—sort of sacred, don't you know? Why, I wouldn't dream of taking my machines away from you!"

The brothers exchanged hopeless looks and walked off, leaving me free to continue in business at River Vista for at least another week.

Even though the Russian River gum venders did uncommonly well, the route failed to maintain the 15-per-cent-a-month increase we had hoped for. Our gross sales climbed to $570 per month, wavered as though panting from the effort, and then fell back. Our "net," after paying commissions and merchandise costs, was around $200, and any boob can clearly see that it's impossible to cover auto expense, taxes, licenses, and other little incidentals like food, rent, and wine, with the sum of $200. Each month, therefore, we had to dip into our shrinking bank account to make up the balance of our spending. And each month we began to think harder and harder about how to increase our earnings—without, of course, increasing our investment.

On a trip to San Francisco in early July, I heard about carded goods. Dilley Stark, a husky ex-nut-machine-operator who had gone to work part-time for No-Name, told me about them. Dilley was a pleasant chap about twenty-eight years old, built along the lines of a large chimpanzee. His hands hung nearly to his knees, and I would guess the distance between his hairline and his eyebrows at roughly five-eighths of an inch. Dilley was clearly distinguishable from the chimpanzee, however, in that he was red-haired, wore clothes, and shaved occasionally. He appeared to be the only non-play-actor at No-Name, and I quickly grew quite fond of him.

Dilley had originally added a line of carded goods to his nut-machine route, he told me, just to pay for his gasoline. However, the carded-goods end of his business had mushroomed to the point where now it actually accounted for about half of his net.

"Just what *are* carded goods?" I asked Freddie.

"You know," he said, waving a limp paw, "jerky, and that stuff."

"Jerky?" I said questioningly.

"My God!" Dilley said. "Ain't you ever been in a bar?"

"I've been in lots of bars," I said defensively, as though my manhood had been challenged, "but I still don't know what jerky is."

Dilley sighed and set down the nut machine he was repairing.

"Carded goods," he said, "is that stuff . . . well, look. There's twenty-four little cellophane sacks full of jerky stapled to this card, see. The card's about the size of a shirt cardboard—only a little smaller, maybe, and stiffer. On the back there's this flange, see, so you can stand the card up."

"Like an easel?"

"That's it," Dilley said, "like an easel. Okay. So I sell a card to the barkeep. He staples it to the wall up behind the bar—he don't want none of his customers reaching themselves a sack of jerky without paying for it, see. And then he sells it, a dime a sack. Twenty-four dimes is $2.40. He pays me $1.70 for the card; I buy the card for about $1.30."

"So what does the customer do with the jerky, once he's got it?"

"Honest to God!" Dilley exclaimed, looking toward the ceiling. "He eats it, that's what he does! Jerky is to eat. It's dried beef, all salted and peppered up and dried. It goes good with beer."

"Oh-h-h-h," I said. "I get it."

"The barkeep likes it, too. It makes the customers thirsty, see. I mean, you eat one of them sacks of jerky, you just gotta have another glass of beer!"

"I follow."

Dilley lifted his left arm slightly and scratched the armpit with his right hand.

"There's other stuff, too," he said, "fried pork skins, dried shrimp, smoked salmon, pretzels, fire-sticks . . ."

"What's a fire-stick?"

"Looks like a skinny cigar," Dilley said. "Kind of crooked. Sort of a dried beef sausage. And hot? Man!"

"Doesn't this stuff have to be refrigerated?"

"Nah. It's all dried or smoked or something. Keeps forever."

I liked Dilley. I was particularly fond of him when he casually dropped the name of his supplier. As soon as I had concluded my meager business with No-Name, I scurried directly to this supplier, the Hotchkiss Nut Company, and invested twenty-five dollars in a carded-goods inventory. It seemed like a lead-pipe cinch.

I realized, of course, that my setup wasn't as favorable as Dilley's. For instance, my machines were mostly in grocery stores, rather than in bars, the way Dilley's were. Thus, instead of merely offering a new sideline to my old customers, I was going to have to dig up a whole raft of new customers—all in bars and cocktail lounges. But so what, I thought? I had to cruise Sonoma and Napa counties once a week anyhow, and I passed by plenty of bars. Instead of driving right by, I might as well stop in and fill their orders for carded goods. I knew that once I had the bartenders lined up as regular customers, it wouldn't take much extra time.

"Child," I told Mary-Armour, as I walked up the front steps that night, "you are now in the carded-goods business."

"The *what* business?"

We sat down in the living room, and I explained everything just the way good old Dilley Stark had told it to me. Mary-Armour's reaction was nothing if not basic.

"Let's sample the merchandise," she said.

We selected a card of beef jerky, each tore off an envelope, and bit into it.

"Mmmmm, not bad," Mary-Armour said. "Spicy, salty, chewy—not bad."

I went to the icebox, got two cans of beer, opened them, and returned. We each took a second envelope of jerky from the card.

"Say, what's this?" Mary-Armour said.

"What's what?"

"Under these envelopes—there's a picture!"

Sure enough, there was a picture. And *what* a picture! At first it appeared to be merely a naked ankle and a fragment of bare shoulder, but even the dimmest peasant could have guessed that there were other unclothed segments of girl connected to those already visible.

"I'll attend to this," Mary-Armour said. "You hide your eyes."

Through my interlaced fingers, as Mary-Armour pulled the remaining sacks off the card, I saw a brilliant color photograph of a girl emerge. The girl, of course, was nude. Like most nude girls in color photos, she was talking on a gold telephone.

The crass, commercial idea that led the manufacturer to place the girl's photograph behind the jerky, of course, was that Joe Customer, having uncovered one part of the girl's anatomy and having had one beer, would become eager to uncover other, racier sections of the card. To do this it was obviously necessary to eat more jerky. More jerky meant more beer. Eventually, after choking down a peck of jerky and a firkin of suds, Joe would have emptied the card of merchandise, and the girl with the long blond mane would be sitting before him, completely naked except for Mr. Bell's invention.

"We can't sell this stuff!" Mary-Armour said indignantly.

"Why not?"

"It's . . . it's pornography!"

"It is not!" I said. "It's art."

Mary-Armour glared at me.

"Okay," I said, "so it's pornography. So what do we do?"

"We eat the merchandise ourselves," Mary-Armour said, "and burn the cards."

"That's twenty-five bucks worth of stuff!" I protested.

"It doesn't matter," Mary-Armour said with finality.

"We're not selling carded goods unless we can get some manufacturer to make up cards without pictures!"

This admirable decision of Mary-Armour's was made at night.

By the dawn's early light, however, economics over-balanced propriety. Therefore, while Mary-Armour looked the other way, I stuffed a batch of carded merchandise into the back of the Jeep, along with my gum equipment, and set off to round up some customers.

I started my quest on the main drinking street of Napa. I was disappointed to find, after my first half-dozen calls, that each tavern already had a perfectly satisfactory supplier of jerky, fried pork skins, and other bar goodies.

I began to work my way up the Napa Valley. Between calls on bars, I carried out my routine servicing of gum machines. By noon I was behind schedule on servicing and had not lined up a single carded-goods customer.

Finally, just outside Guerneville, I hit what I will give the courtesy title of pay dirt. A kindly gray-haired bartender bought two cards of merchandise and consented to be my steady customer all summer. Near the Sebastopol apple-packing plant I found another customer, like the first a little bit off the beaten track and therefore not spoken for by some other jerky merchant. A week later I found a third customer, on Highway 101, so new at barkeeping that no carded-goods vender had got to him yet.

These three accounts formed the Carded Goods Division of Multivend Industries. I called on them assiduously each week during the summer months. Carrying these added lines of merchandise, of course, meant lugging a big box full of cards around with me every time I went out, and it also meant one more supplier to call on each time I went to San Francisco. (We eventually found a supplier, incidentally, whose cards had slightly more restrained pictures under the jerky envelopes, which made Mary-

Armour happy and didn't seem to affect the sale of jerky much one way or the other.) During the hottest days of summer, some of the pepperoni sausages went moldy, and I had to give refunds. The smoked salmon did what is known in the carded-goods trade as "sweating," and discolored some of the other cards so that they had to be offered at a cut price. But there were no machines to jam, tip over, or get scratched. In fact, the only complaint I could make about the carded-goods business was that there wasn't enough of it.

The summer wore on. Once every two or three weeks I Jeeped into San Francisco to get merchandise. I always enjoyed these trips, especially when Mary-Armour could go with me. The city was cool in the summer, and it was nice now and then to sample something other than the warmth of Sonoma County. We always managed to work in a cheap lunch in Chinatown, too, which put us in such a good frame of mind that we never minded being stopped on the way home by a drawbridge or by a long freight train at the Highway 101 junction. In fact, we started a collection of the fine old railroad phrases stenciled on the sides of the cars, such as "Bolster Snubber Springs," and "1-W-WROT Steel Wheels."

On one particularly chilly summer day in San Francisco, I stumbled onto a new supplier, the Roland Skillman Company. It was pure accident; I just happened to be driving past the store and saw the jumble of second-hand gum machines in the window.

I parked the Jeep and stood for a long time outside the store, examining the front window display. Then I finally walked in. There was only one person in the crowded little store, a spare, elderly gentleman in a stiff collar, a bowtie, a conservative gray suit, and spats. He turned out to be old Mr. Skillman himself. He was talking on the phone when I entered.

"No," he said into the mouthpiece, "pigeons. Not pinches—pigeons. Like birds. You know."

I began to look at Skillman's charm supply. He had several varieties I'd never seen before. Since No-Name's charm supply hadn't changed once in the six months I'd been in business, I was pleased to discover a few new items.

"No, no!" the old gentleman yelled into the phone. "I said *pigeons!* P-i-g-e-o-n-s. Yes, that's right, pigeons."

I continued to look at the charms, the used cigarette machines stacked along the wall, the merchandise price lists stapled to the storeroom door. At last the old man hung up the phone and approached me.

"What can I do for you, young man?" he inquired.

"What do you have in the way of charms?" I asked.

"Nothing's in the way, son," he said. "You can get right to 'em!" He cackled appreciatively. "That's an old one," he said.

I tried to insert a look of forbearance in my smile.

Skillman pulled open a drawer under the counter and withdrew a tiny set of false teeth. "Have you seen these?" he asked. "Hottest charm on the market. One or two of these in a globe will empty it right away!"

"That so?"

"Absolutely!" His tone of voice left no room for doubt. I began to pick up a bit of his enthusiasm.

"Kids really go for them, eh?"

"I have one customer sells 'em, nickel apiece. Fixed up a machine that vends 'em straight. Kids buy out his machine in no time."

"How much are they?"

"Two cents apiece."

"I'll take a hundred," I said. I was feeling pretty good about stumbling into this place. It looked as though I'd solved a lot of my problems by finding a place where I could buy charms that would really *pull.*

"Anything else?"

"Yes," I said, "do you raise pigeons? I couldn't help overhearing your telephone conversation."

The old man threw his head back and laughed. "Lord, no!" he said. "I don't raise 'em—I buy 'em out."

"You buy pigeons out?" I said. "I don't get it."

"Don't you know what a pigeon is?"

"I guess not."

"It's one of these fellows who gets taken in by a sharpie—buys penny machines for forty, fifty, sixty dollars apiece."

I swallowed hard and nodded, doing my best to look unpigeonlike.

"In other words, a sucker," Skillman said. He winked at me slyly. "There's one born every minute, you know."

"I know," I said.

Two days later I got a batch of false-teeth charms into circulation, and a week after that I knew the awful truth: no one liked my new charms except the storekeepers. They were crazy about them.

"Next time around, bring me a set, will you?" If I heard it once, I heard it twenty times.

In San Francisco a couple of weeks later, I called on Skillman again.

"How'd the teeth do?" he asked me.

"Awful," I said.

Skillman looked surprised. "Don't understand that," he said. "But maybe it just wasn't the right time for them. Maybe after school starts, eh? Meanwhile—here's the hottest charm of the century. Look—a ship in a bottle!"

It really was a handsome little charm. I bought heavily after Skillman gave me the customary assurance that one or two in a globe would empty it quicker than you could say Roland Skillman Company, Vending Machine Suppliers.

The result of the ship-in-bottle charm, of course, was

that the storekeepers thought it was magnificent, and would I mind bringing them a couple for their two daughters next time out, and maybe another, if I had it, for their niece. And meanwhile, the Boston Bean machines ground along at the same slow, steady pace.

In time, of course, I learned to resist the compelling salestalk of Skillman, the genial old pitchman. I came to know all his refrains, but the one I loved best was the one in which he told me, each time I called, "Yes, sir, I made a lot of money from gum machines. Put three children through college that way. Remember the old Pulver machine? That was my machine. It had a little man who turned and dropped a ball of gum down the escape slot. That was a real machine! Ball gum cost ten cents a pound in those days, and there was *real* money in it!"

Ball gum cost twenty-nine to thirty-one cents a pound during my trick at the helm, and the prospects of putting Jamie through college on the proceeds from our machines looked exceedingly dim. In fact, everything financial was looking dimmer and dimmer. It had become possible to calculate the exact day when, due to our regular monthly withdrawals, our savings account would be completely empty. The specter of honest, five-day-a-week employment hung ominously over my head.

To stave that day off as long as possible, Mary-Armour and I combed our operation more feverishly than ever to see if there wasn't something we were doing wrong, some aspect of the business we were neglecting.

On a Friday night in July I arrived home from a day of collecting pennies, to find Mary-Armour waiting breathlessly on the front steps. The minute I stopped the Jeep, she was standing by the car door, her face radiant with excitement.

"What's up with you?" I asked. "Did you win the sweepstakes?"

Mary-Armour leaned through the Jeep window and kissed me fervently.

"Oh, God, we're so *dumb!*" she said.

"If you want to include me in that statement," I said, opening the door and stepping out, "you'll have to explain."

Cleo came bounding across the lawn, knocking Jamie down, and jumped up on me. Miraculously enough, her paws were not muddy. It seemed as though they reached to my shoulders.

"We've been blind!" Mary-Armour said. "Absolutely blind to our opportunities!"

"What opportunities?"

"Look," she said, "how many pennies do we handle in a month's time?"

"Well, about four hundred or five hundred dollars worth," I said.

"How many pennies is that?"

"That's . . . forty or fifty thousand, I guess."

"And how much are they worth apiece?"

"Quit being so cryptic," I said, "and get down to cases."

"All right. We handle fifty thousand pennies a month, and most of them are worth one cent apiece. Right? But did you ever hear of Victor D. Brenner?"

"Darling, you need a rest," I said. "You stay in bed tomorrow, and I'll—"

"Victor D. Brenner designed the Lincoln-head penny," Mary-Armour said. "In 1909. I heard it on this program today, over the radio."

"So?"

"So he put his initials on it, and a whole lot of them got issued before anyone noticed it. And then Congress or somebody decided that pennies looked better without Mr. Brenner's initials on them, so they tried to recall them. But of course there were a bunch of them in circulation already, and people hung onto them, because they knew they'd be collectors' items. And do you know what a good V.D.B. penny sells for in a coin store nowadays?"

"How much?"

"Up to twenty-five dollars!"

"No kidding," I said.

"That's if it has an 'S' mint mark," Mary-Armour said. "And do you know what a 1914 penny brings—without any V.D.B. or anything—just a plain old 1914 penny with a 'D' mint mark?"

"How much?"

"Sixty dollars!"

"Sixty bucks? For a Lincoln-head penny?"

"I wrote it all down," Mary-Armour said. 'There are some others, too—1923, 1924, 1931—they all have bounties on them. Now do you begin to see where we've been missing the boat?"

"Sweetie, I've got to hand it to you," I said. "I never would have thought of that! Why, out of fifty thousand pennies, there must be—I mean, just thinking of the law of averages—there must be quite a few that must be worth, if not sixty bucks, at least five or ten or, well, at *least* a buck!"

"Sure there are, loads of them!" Mary-Armour said.

We had a bottle of Mr. Montreux's wine with dinner that night, in celebration of finding the key to the whole penny-gum business. After dinner we made duplicate copies of the list Mary-Armour had copied down from the radio program. Mary-Armour wanted to get started right away.

"Now wait a minute," I said. "Let's take it easy. The coins aren't going to change dates and mint marks overnight. Let's relax and enjoy our evening according to our master plan, and leave the money-grubbing till morning."

So we sat down and played a game of Go, which is a centuries-old Japanese game we had learned on the East

Coast. Ordinarily we were pretty evenly matched, but this evening I won easily, because Mary-Armour was trying to memorize her penny list.

The next morning Mary-Armour and I put on our dark glasses and took fifty dollars' worth of pennies out into the hot sunshine to get rich and sunburned simultaneously. Each of us had a big tray onto which we scooped a few handfuls of pennies for examination. Naturally, about half the pennies spread out on the trays had to be turned over, since they had landed tail-side up.

We hunted in silence for about five minutes.

"Hey, hey, hey!" Mary-Armour shouted suddenly. "Eureka! I've found one on the list!"

I set my own tray down hurriedly and began looking over her shoulder.

"Nineteen thirty-one," she said. "Mint mark 'S.' How much is it worth?"

I picked up her list. "What shape is it in?"

"Awful."

"In mint condition it's worth $1.75," I said.

"Well, this one ought to bring what—a quarter? Half a dollar? A dollar?"

I took the coin and looked at it. The date was barely visible. Time and a million grubby hands had almost rubbed Mr. Lincoln off the face.

"Never mind what it's worth," I said. "It's worth more than a penny, we know that. Now let's find a whole lot more like it."

Five minutes later I heard Mary-Armour squeal a second time.

"Eureka again! I've got another!" Her voice was jubilant. "Why didn't we think of this before?"

"What have you got this time?"

" 'S' mint mark. 1923. What's it worth?"

"What shape is it in?"

"Same as the first."

I consulted the list. "About fifty cents," I said.

"How long have we been looking?" Mary-Armour asked.

"About ten minutes."

"Two coins in ten minutes—not bad!" she said. "We've already made $1.25. Why, if we can find two of these every ten minutes, we've got it made!"

During the next two hours and thirty-five minutes, however, we found no more coins on the list.

"All I see is spots," Mary-Armour said finally. "Let's go inside."

That afternoon we continued our search—in the shade this time—and that evening, seated around the big kitchen table, we searched some more. By the time we went to bed, we had processed $310—that's 31,000 pennies, in case you're interested—and we still had only Mary-Armour's two initial finds for our pains.

The following morning we processed an additional fifty dollars and gave up. Our eyeballs were spinning, and we felt sure that the fee of the ophthalmologist we were going to need would far exceed the reward for any valuable pennies we might find. Thus our careers as numismatists came to an abrupt and melancholy close.

12

As summer drew to a close, I decided that our financial salvation lay in my making and selling linoleum-block Christmas cards. For the preceding five or six years I had always turned out a card that drew favorable comments from our friends (does anyone ever tell the maker of a home-made Christmas card that his work stinks?) and, based on this small critical approval, I decided to launch a new, life-saving business venture.

While the August sun poured the heat on, I sat outdoors with my linoleum blocks and pencils and paper and Exacto knives and tried to think up clever Christmassy thoughts. Jamie and Cleo frisked about my knees, and Mary-Armour kept me supplied with lemonade.

Let's see, what do I have to work with, I asked myself. Pine trees, candles, the manger scene, Santa Claus, reindeer, snow . . .

The first linoleum block took me from Monday through Saturday to complete—I redid it four times—and it was awful. Even Mary-Armour, who usually looks on my artistic creations with a friendly, encouraging eye, had a hard time being enthusiastic.

On Sunday morning—we were going to sleep late and give ourselves a holiday—we were awakened by a thunderous roar that shook every timber in the house. We both leapt out of bed, Mary-Armour to run and comfort Jamie, who had begun to scream bloody murder, and I to go outside and see what had caused the noise.

Clad only in my pajamas and slippers, I ran out on the lawn in time to see a small, sleek, silver airplane banking deeply over the vicinity of Simmons' house. As I watched, it completed its turn and began to swoop directly toward me. The engine whined as the pilot poured on the coal for another run.

Suddenly it came to me. Jotto Baker! The liquor and delicatessen king! He was making good on his promise to "give your kid a treat."

The house, the trees, the earth—everything seemed to tremble as he came diving with his throttle wide open. I held my breath; I thought he was going to crash into our roof! Then at the last moment he pulled up, just in time to avoid the oak trees, and went shooting off in the direction of Sonoma.

Mary-Armour appeared on the front porch in her bathrobe, holding Jamie in her arms. "What is it," she shouted.

"One of our customers," I shouted back.

"Good Lord!" Mary-Armour said, starting back into the house. "What did you ever do to him?"

Jotto's engine whined again. As I turned around, he swooped noisily across the house. I could see his faded blue hat through the plane's canopy. He circled Simmons' place and headed back at me once more. I waved my arms frantically, trying to signal "go away" to him but . . . well, *you* try signaling "go away" to a power-mad liquor store-delicatessen operator who is making runs on you at a hundred and some miles per hour!

Finally I just gave up. I dragged a bench from under the biggest oak into the sunshine and sat down and watched. Jotto must have kept up his aerial circus for at least ten minutes; it seemed like about two hours. Then I heard the roar of another motor, and Simmons appeared, riding up our drive on his motorcycle. As he skidded his motorcycle to a halt, I saw that he had a double-barreled shotgun across his handlebars. Briefly I wondered what he had been hunting at this season of the year.

The airplane made another reverberating pass. Simmons and I both ducked involuntarily.

"Crazy damn fool!" Simmons said, shaking one fist in the air. He dismounted and walked into the middle of our lawn carrying the shotgun. "Rabbits all runnin' around like they was crazy, and chickens won't lay for a month now!" he said. He looked up and shaded his eyes from the sun with his left hand.

The accelerating whine of Jotto's engine told me that he was coming through again. My eyes opened wide as I saw Simmons put the gun to his shoulder.

"Mr. Simmons!" I shouted. On came the screaming silver plane. Ka-powie! One barrel. Ka-powie! The other. The plane veered sharply to the left and shot upward in a stiff climb.

Simmons broke the gun, ejected the two spent cartridges onto our drive and reloaded. He raised the gun again. Ka-powie! Ka-powie! But the plane, still climbing, was now out of range.

"That'll teach *that* sonofabitch!" Simmons said, lowering the gun.

I was too stunned to speak.

Simmons broke the gun once more and ejected the shells. Then he climbed back on his motorcycle and started up the engine.

I finally regained my voice.

"Great Scott, Mr. Simmons!" I said. "You might have—"

"No need to thank me," he said genially, waving his hand. "Did it as much for my own sake as for yours."

Simmons' motorcycle threw up a shower of gravel as he blasted off down the drive. Then, finally, after the minute and a half it took him to zoom down the road to his own house, there was absolute, complete, blessed quiet.

I began my second week of cardmaking by reading Dickens' *Christmas Carol*. It produced no ideas. I spent another whole morning rummaging around the house, trying to find a cardboard box reputed to contain all the cards we had received the preceding Christmas. All I found was a stack of four-year-old San Francisco *Chronicles,* and before I knew it, I'd frittered away most of the afternoon looking at them.

"I must be out of my mind," I said to Mary-Armour that night, "thinking I can make Christmas cards anyone would pay good money for!"

"Why, of course you can," Mary-Armour said reprovingly. "You just haven't hit your stride yet."

By the end of August I still hadn't hit my stride. And as I tried, day after day, to turn out some suitable designs, red gum machines were piling up in our storeroom.

During an ordinary period, I would have spent a few days finding new homes for these machines, and thus have kept them in service. But the Christmas-card deal was an all-out effort, so I contented myself with giving the route the briefest of weekly attentions. And that, of course, meant no relocating.

And still the machines came home to roost. Mostly they did so because some store had changed hands, and the new owner happened to abhor gum machines. Or else, without the slightest warning, some business would disappear from the scene entirely. The rate at which these two phenomena took place amazed me. I had grocery stores that changed hands overnight, restaurants that went bankrupt right in the middle of the tourist season, two soda fountains that were seized for nonpayment of federal taxes, and one pool hall that changed hands five times in less than a year.

And then suddenly it was the Wednesday after Labor Day, and time for me to lay aside my linoleum blocks and make another hurried trip around the route.

Everyone was up early that morning to help Daddy get off to a good early start. While the coffee was perking and Mary-Armour was wrestling Jamie into a sunsuit, I opened the back door and whistled for Cleo. There was no response.

"Cleo!" I shouted. "Here, Cleo-eo-eo!"

Ordinarily she came bounding up the back steps, eager to get in and begin knocking things over. But this morning she was nowhere to be found.

Mary-Armour brought Jamie to the kitchen and dumped him in his high chair.

"Have you seen Cleo?" I asked.

"No. Is she missing?"

"I guess so," I said. "I'll take a look around in front."

I stepped out the back door into the gorgeous sunshine and walked around to the front of the house, calling Cleo's name. And then I saw her, lying with her nose between her paws on the front porch. The porch was made of broad boards set side by side with open half-inch slots between them. You could crawl right under it, if you wanted, and Jamie spent a lot of time playing in its shade.

Cleo's tail thumped feebly at my approach.

"What's the matter, old girl?" I asked. "Here, come here." I held out my hand. Cleo gave a wiggle as though she were trying to get up, but couldn't. She didn't move an inch from her place.

"My God!" I said, bounding up the steps in alarm. "What's the matter, Cleo?" I shouted into the house. "Sweetie, come quickly!"

Mary-Armour appeared at the front door on the double. "What's the matter?"

"Something's wrong with Cleo," I said. "She can't move."

"She's been hit by a car!" Mary-Armour said. "Oh, the poor, poor dog!" She knelt beside Cleo and stroked her very gently.

"No," I said, "she'd be bloody if she'd been hit by a car, and she's not. Here, let me pick her up—we'll take her inside."

I put my arms under her fore and hindquarters and started to lift. Cleo yelped in pain before I had moved her an inch.

"Don't move her!" Mary-Armour said. "She's dislocated something. It kills her to move."

It did seem that Cleo's legs projected out from her body at crazy angles. And she had a bump on her back—had that always been there, or was it new? Without lifting her head from the porch Cleo looked up at us sadly.

"I'll get her some water," Mary-Armour said.

"I'll erect a sunshade," I said. "It's going to get pretty hot out here before long. But first I'd better phone the vet."

"Yes, do that first, by all means," Mary-Armour said fervently.

The breakfast bacon had burned to a crisp in the kitchen, but we didn't care. I dialed Dr. Flamenco's number—he lived seven miles away—and got his wife who said that Dr. Flamenco had gone out at 5:00 A.M. to doctor some sick sheep and wouldn't be back till ten o'clock.

I looked at my watch. That was three hours away.

"Tell him right away when he gets home, please," I said. "It's an emergency—our dog can't even move!"

Cleo would drink no water, eat no dog food. She just lay there and looked up at us mournfully. We put up the sunshade and petted her. Jamie came out and rubbed his face in her fur, but nothing could make her move her head or any part of her body.

"I'll just *die* if anything happens to her," Mary-Armour said.

"Don't worry, sweetie," I said, but the fact was I felt none too confident about a dog that couldn't even lift its head.

It was a long, agonizing morning. We all went around with long faces. My own thoughts were concerned with what we should do if Cleo . . . well, went west, so to speak. We should get another dog right away, I decided; it would be best all around.

One of us stayed with Cleo constantly, to keep the poor dog company. Her condition didn't seem to be worsening, actually, but it wasn't improving, either. Her nose remained glued to the porch.

At 10:15, when Dr. Flamenco still hadn't shown up, I went indoors and phoned again. He hadn't come back yet, Mrs. Flamenco said; she'd tell him the very first minute . . .

"Where on earth do you suppose he is?" I asked Mary-Armour. She merely shut her eyes and shook her head slowly.

At 10:30, I stood up to call again.

"He'll come as soon as he can," Mary-Armour said.

I sat down again. And then I noticed that Mary-Armour was kneeling on the porch, with her head down on the level of Cleo's.

"What do you see?" I asked.

"Oh, for goodness sakes!" Mary-Armour said. She stood up and put her hands on her hips in disgust.

"What is it?" I said.

"Look, her collar is caught between two of these boards," she said. "That's all that's the matter with her."

Mary-Armour walked down the steps and around to the side of the porch. Crouching slightly, she went under the porch and straightened the two tags—license and rabies —that hung down between the slats from Cleo's collar chain. Cleo lifted her head, the tags came up through the slats, and she was a free dog once more. She bolted down the steps and out into the bushes, where she relieved herself at some length. Then she returned, bounding up the steps in the best of spirits and licking Jamie mercilessly.

Our relief was enormous. Mary-Armour and I clutched one another, laughing weakly.

After a moment, Mary-Armour stiffened. "The vet!" she said. "Better see if you can head him off before he drives all the way out here!"

I sprinted to the phone and dialed Dr. Flamenco's number.

"I'm *sorry*, Mr. Nelson," Mrs. Flamenco said, her patience sounding a bit thin, "I *told* you I'd tell him as soon as he got here . . ."

For a second time, I felt relief—relief that he wasn't on his expensive way out to our house. With considerable circumlocution, I explained to Mrs. Flamenco that we'd done one or two little things for the dog, and that the dog seemed to feel quite a bit better. In fact, there was no reason for the doctor to trouble himself driving all the way out to our place when it looked as though the crisis were past.

"Well, you call again if the dog takes a turn for the worse," Mrs. Flamenco said, and I said yes indeed, by all means, I most certainly would.

Gone, of course, was the early start on a day of servicing, but I decided to make the most of what was left. I loaded the Jeep, kissed wife and child, and headed down the road toward my first stop, Ben Thurlow's shoe-shine stand.

The stand wasn't occupied, but when I opened the machine I discovered a wadded-up note lying on top of the coin box. How Ben got it in there, I don't know. I smoothed it out in my fingers and began to read.

"Dear Mr. Nelson," it said. "I will not be opening the stand for about a week, as I am having trouble with the newspaper. The district attorney told me I would have to get a license just like the *Daily Reporter-Bugle* or else quit publishing. Sincerely yours, Benjamin R. Thurlow."

I gathered that Ben's editorial arrows had been landing in City Hall again.

At Wing Duck's I found my tiny friend Freddie nervously hopping from one foot to the other as he supervised Moonstone's labors. She was engaged in restacking an already perfectly stacked shelf of sardines, smoked oysters, and kippered herring. Freddie gave me what had become his standard greeting.

"Hoz Leo?"

"Cleo's fine," I said, "but she made me waste a lot of time this morning. And the other day she tried to eat a neighbor's chicken."

Freddie grabbed his head with both hands and walked to the cash register.

"That's bad," he said. Thrusting his hands into his pockets, he mounted his Bongo Board and began to see-saw back and forth. His face brightened.

"Know how to cure chicken-dog?" he asked.

"Well, I've had quite a few suggestions," I said. "One man told me to beat the dog with a dead chicken, and someone else said to tie the chicken around the dog's neck and leave it there for a month."

"Nah, nah, no good," Freddie said, shaking his head.

"Okay, Freddie," I said, "what's your system?"

"Dip chickens in creosote," Freddie said. "Then dog leave 'em alone."

"Creosote!" I said. "Good Lord, that would kill the chickens!"

Freddie cocked his head on one side and nodded judiciously. "But dog sure leave 'em alone, you betcha!" he said.

At Henry Skill's Supermarket I had almost finished servicing the machines when I saw Henry himself. As I passed him on the way out, I said "Good morning."

Apparently he was in one of his better moods, because instead of spitting, snarling, or kicking at me, he merely replied gruffly, "Yeah?"

Oh, I tell you, he was feeling grand!

As I entered The Frog Hollow Delicatessen, I heard a throaty baritone rendition of *"Adios, Amigos Compañeros de mi Vida."* The singer, Joe Lopez y Garcia, was sitting on the shelf behind his cash register, massaging the back of his neck with his hand. I noted with interest that he had begun to regrow his mustache.

"Yeah," he replied cordially, "I decided it wasn't so goddam unsanitary after all. That's the way with us goddam manic-depressives—we keep changing our goddam minds."

"Well, I'm glad you're so goddam manic," I said.

Joe chuckled. "Yeah, me too," he said. He picked up a can off the shelf and handed it to me. "Ever try these canned tamales? This brand's just about as close as you can come to the real thing in a can."

"That so?" I said. "I'll have to try them. How much?"

"It's on the goddam house today," Joe said. Before I could thank him, he turned and started toward the back of the store, singing lustily, *"Adiós, amigos compañeros . . ."*

I found Tanaka Watanabe's store closed up tight. By peering through the front window, however, I was able to see his slender, dark-haired granddaughter at the back of the store. She wore her customary uniform—white rubber-soled shoes, bobby-sox, pleated skirt, sloppy oversized sweater, and a string of fake pearls. She looked up when I knocked on the window, and came to the door. She looked very serious, and I realized suddenly that I had almost never seen her when she wasn't giggling.

"You better take your machine," she said. Over her shoulder I saw her tiny, dignified grandfather walking toward us.

"You closing the store?" I asked the girl.

"Grandpa must go out of business," she said solemnly. "He is losing the store, and he is losing the truck garden. We have nothing left except our little house."

Old Mr. Watanabe arrived at the door, opened it wide, and bowed.

"Won't you come in?" he said.

"I'm terribly sorry to hear . . ." I began, but Mr. Watanabe held up his hand.

"If you will kindly weigh the pennies from the machine and give our share to my granddaughter," he said quietly, "I will see that they are turned over to the proper persons."

"Yes, sir," I said.

"Thank you."

Mr. Watanabe bowed again, and I found myself bowing in return. As Mr. Watanabe walked to the rear of the store, Mary-Lou burst into tears.

"He has worked so *hard!*" she said helplessly.

There was seventy-three cents in the machine. Mr. Watanabe's share was fifteen cents.

I removed the globe of bubble gum from the machine, preparatory to loading the machine into my car. I held the globe out to Mary Lou.

"Get a little sack," I said, "and fish out some of the orange ones."

Mary-Lou started to cry again, so I got a sack myself and put a couple of dozen orange gumballs in it and gave it to her, and left, feeling very much depressed.

I reached the Russian River just after lunch. A week previous, the area had been bursting with vacationers. Today, two days after Labor Day, it couldn't have been deader. Some of the proprietors had already gone, and others were boarding their places up for the winter. In a Guerneville drugstore where I stopped for a Coke, I sat on a stool next to a summer grocer. He was moaning about how bad the season had been. I offered some condolences.

"Really a rough season, eh?" I said.

"Rough as a cob," he said. "Really rotten. Why, the wife and I were planning to spend the winter in Mexico. Now we're having to cut our trip to ten weeks!"

I thought ruefully of poor, uncomplaining Mr. Watanabe.

"Business *must* have been lousy," I said.

"Of course, I always have a little extra vacation money," the grocer said, winking at me evilly, "even in a bad season, because every time I get a silver dollar in the store, I toss it in a special bucket. You don't really miss it from the cash register, and the government don't miss it, either. Saved about $1,300 that way this year."

I slipped a little arsenic into his coffee and went about my business, pulling the Russian River machines off location and skedaddling around the rest of the route.

At about two-forty-five in the afternoon, one of my carded-goods customers told me that I might as well forget about selling him any more jerky. He'd lost his beer and wine license for selling to a minor.

"Biggest sonofabitching minor I ever seen!" he bellowed at me. "Six-feet-four if he was an inch! Two hundred and ten pounds! My God, I'd a' swore he was thirty!"

At three-fifteen, a second carded-goods customer gave me the air.

"Going out of business," he told me happily. "Day after tomorrow I'm old enough for the pension."

I wished him a happy birthday and pushed on, wondering about the advisability of discontinuing the carded-goods division. Forty-five minutes later I approached my one remaining jerky-buying stop.

"Fritz," I said to the proprietor, "I'm closing out my entire stock of carded goods at twenty per cent off. Why don't you buy up the whole shooting match and turn yourself into a rich man?"

"You're going out of business?" he asked.

"Out of the carded-goods business," I said. "I'll still have my machines."

Fritz considered for a moment.

"Well, I'm pretty well stocked right now," he said. "That stuff hasn't been moving too well."

"How about thirty per cent off?"

Fritz shook his head. "I'm the only one around here eats much of the darn stuff," he said, "and I don't make a hell of a lot out of me."

That night Mary-Armour came up with the perfect solution to the carded-goods problem. "We'll give a party," she said, "and use the remaining inventory for hors d'oeuvres."

A week later we did, and it was a huge success, too—jerky, blondes, and all.

Relocating the machines that had come from the Russian River was no chore at all, of course. I merely took them back to the school locations where they'd spent the spring and put them back to work. But quite apart from these, I now had fifteen non-producing machines sitting in the storeroom.

All of a sudden—possibly because I began to fret over the possibility of having all hundred machines land in the storeroom with me—the linoleum-block venture bogged down completely. Every Christmassy thought I ever had left me. Four times in one morning I cut myself with my knife. It looked like a good time to gird my loins once again for the distasteful job of finding new homes for my orphan machines.

Hell, according to my way of thinking, is a place where there is an infinite number of gum machines and a finite number of locations. That's the way I felt about it, anyhow, as I began to polish and reload and repair my homeless venders and start the hunt for new locations.

Good morning, my name is Jim Nelson. I operate a small route of vending machines and . . . oh, is that so? I see, well thanks anyway. . . . Good morning, my name is Jim Nelson. I live in Sonoma and operate a small route of . . . now wait a minute—there's no need to get nasty! . . . Good morning, my name is . . .

It was during this period that I stumbled onto hairy-eared old J. B. Grommet, the Napa Valley grocer whose insouciant attitude led me to lock him in his washroom. This action on my part led me to indulge in a period of what has become popularly known as "agonizing reappraisal." I considered what was happening to the business, and I considered what was happening to me. And I considered, on the one hand, how failure—when it happens to the right sort of chap, anyhow—merely spurs him on to try, try again; for me, the only reaction was a desire to quit, quit entirely.

I would have quit, too, if I hadn't known that to quit was to chuck our poorly invested little nest egg of $5,256 for ever and ever out the window.

So I kept on plugging, aided by the law of averages, which is a very fine law indeed, and states that if you call on enough grocers, gas stations, drugstores, and restaurants, you will eventually place a gum machine. This law holds no matter who you are or what your machine looks like, and it was the salvation of the Multivend Company.

My new locations were not exactly prime, but by God they got the machines out of the storeroom! I put two in a grocery so ancient that I felt sure the building would collapse before I could get back for my first service call. I placed another in a town so small that I knew, even before I made my pitch to the owner, that the coin box would collect only dust. But who cared—the machine was on location, wasn't it?

With considerable amazement, I discovered one noon that I had relocated an even dozen machines. This knowledge encouraged me so much that I decided it was time to try the plywood mills.

Once a week, ever since I'd begun operation, I had driven past two thriving plywood mills near our home, and once a week I had vowed that I would try to place a machine in one of them immediately, maybe even tomorrow. But somehow I never seemed to have the time—or the guts, or the inspiration or something—to go in and make my pitch.

Fortunately, at the time of my big relocating jag, the American Chicle Company came out with a sales-help pamphlet purporting to summarize the findings of a Columbia University professor named Harry L. Hollingworth, who had conducted numerous experiments in "The Psycho-Dynamics of Chewing." After four years of study, and chewing God knows how much gum, Professor Hollingworth had come up with the conclusion that people who chewed gum exerted more energy than people who didn't. ("Whether writing or pushing pins in a board, these operations were done with more vigor than is true in the instance of the same people when not chewing.") They, the chewers, that is, also experienced less tension, suffered less fatigue, and worked faster when they chewed. Although the pamphlet did not go into Nervous Stomach or Nagging Backache, it did point out that persons using pencils pressed down on them harder than those not chewing. (You can tell a gum chewer by the clarity of his second carbon, although, of course, he breaks a lot of points.)

The brochure also pointed out, although it did not lay this at the professor's door, that chewing cut the need for a smoke or a trip to the water cooler. I was so inspired by reading all this that I felt it would be sheer madness for any industrial plant to say "no" to one of my gum dispensers.

The men in the office of the first plywood mill were cordial but not particularly interested in what Professor Hollingworth had to say.

"If you want to cut down trips to the water cooler," I said, "I've got a sure-fire way."

"Frankly, we aren't bothered much by that problem," the foreman told me, fanning himself with a copy of Professor Hollingworth's remarks. "We don't have a water cooler."

"Whether writing or pushing pins in a board," I said nervously, "your men will do it with more vigor if they're chewing gum."

"Listen, sonny," the foreman said, "what are you trying to do, sell me some gum?"

"Great Scott, no!" I said. "I don't want to sell you anything. All I want to do is install a penny-gum machine."

"Why'nt you say so in the first place?" he said. "Sure. Go ahead, put one in."

"Well, thank you," I said. "I'm sure you'll find you've made a wise decision productionwise."

"The hell with production," he said. "I just like to chew."

I postponed calling on the second mill until I could see how the machine in the first was doing. In a week's time, it was half empty. I was delighted. Industrial locations were really okay, I decided. And so I dropped in on the superintendent of the second plant.

"All I can say is," he said, as he gave me the go-ahead, "I sure hope the boys don't wreck your machine for you!"

Two days later, the newly-installed machine in plywood

mill number two was completely empty. I thanked my lucky stars for the plywood industry, and hastily put in another machine.

I was just beginning to feel good about the success of my relocating campaign, just beginning to envision the cutest little Christmas angels carved in linoleum, when tragedy struck.

By tragedy, I mean competition.

Personally, I love competition. I think it's a wonderful thing, especially when it exists between two people selling me the things I want to buy. I mean, that's what made our country great, isn't it? Sure it is. Only, by golly, when someone starts to compete with *me,* that's a gumball of a different color!

The worst part about the whole situation was that the competition's newly located machines were succeeding stupendously. The new operator's machines cost a nickel to play and offered a straight diet of charms. No gumballs, no chocolate peanuts, no inedible Boston Beans. Just charms. Every player a winner.

In my competitor's first load, all the charms were cabochon rings—handsome, silvery rings (even I wanted one!) set with a colorful transparent plastic stone.

The younger set was crazy about them. When I went to Cobwell's Market to service my machines (I needn't have —my rival's machines were doing all the business), I saw some tiny customers with as many as ten rings on their fingers. At the Vista Verde Supermarket, the story was the same. A clerk at the checkout counter told me that the new machine had done twenty-five dollars' worth of business in less than a week. When I looked at the gaudy fingers of the moppets tottering in and out of the store, I could easily believe it.

"We have to *do* something," I told Mary-Armour dejectedly that night. "But what? That's the question."

"The rings are really going over big, are they?"

"Every kid in Santa Rosa has at least one," I said. "And they'll have ten as soon as they can wheedle the money out of their parents."

"Well, why don't we sell rings, too?"

I looked up quickly.

"Us?"

"Why not?"

"Well, I don't know why not," I said. My thoughts were beginning to tumble over one another excitedly. "By golly, you've got it. We'll Fight Back!"

After all, Fighting Back was in the finest tradition of tycoonhood.

I was on Truslow Thomas's doorstep the next morning almost before he opened.

"Truss," I said, "I want to convert some of my machines to nickel operation."

Truss's arched eyebrows and sympathetic smile told me that if it was help I needed, I'd indeed come to the right place.

"Easiest thing in the world, Jim," he said. "You just unscrew three little screws, change the coin wheel, reinsert the three screws, and you're in."

"It's that easy?"

"It's a breeze."

For a price, Truss supplied me with a dozen five-cent coin wheels, and a dozen five-cent nameplates for my machines. He was certain that my converted machines would vend rings without a whimper. And since he didn't handle rings himself, he even suggested a place in Oakland where I could buy them.

The minute I left No-Name, I phoned Mr. Murchie, the Oakland ring supplier. I gave him an order, hurried home to confirm it with a letter and a check, and set about to convert some machines.

I might have guessed that Truss had underplayed the difficulties. Before I could convert even one machine, I was forced to design and manufacture some extra spare parts out of an old coffee can. It took me a full day to get two machines changed over.

Now that I had two machines converted, I had to mark time because the rings hadn't arrived. I didn't want to pull any more machines off location and convert them until I was certain my conversions would actually vend a heavy item like the rings.

I telephoned my polite, elderly supplier, Roland Skillman. Did he have rings? Of course he had rings! Not a metal ring, however, but a fine plastic one, a simulated cameo which was alleged to glow in the dark. "Hottest ring of the century!" I was told by none other than stiff-collared, thumbs-in-vest Roland Skillman himself. I dashed into the city and bought a thousand for sixteen dollars.

That night, Mary-Armour and I sat down around the kitchen table to "load" the rings. Since the rings were of the open-back variety (and adjustable, therefore, to any size finger), it was easy for two rings to become linked. And placed in a globe on a machine, they might—tragedy of all tragedies—vend two for a nickel. What kind of business would that be?

To eliminate this frightening possibility, Mary-Armour and I inserted a marble in the middle of each ring. This gave the finished unit a more or less spherical shape which made it pass through the machine more easily, a procedure we had copied from our ring-vending competitor. Fortunately, we just happened to have a thousand marbles on hand, left over from a previous experiment in which we had tried, unsuccessfully, to vend them at the beginning of marble season for a penny apiece.

Loading was an easy, but a time-consuming job, and it took one heck of a lot of rings to fill a globe. The worst problem was to make the marbles stay in the rings, and before we were through, we had to strap each marble into its ring with Scotch tape. By working until well past midnight, we were able to load almost a globeful.

The following day I dashed four miles to the New California Market in Sonoma and hopefully installed a machine full of rings. I pasted a little sign on the front of the machine calling the customers' attention to the fact that the rings glowed in the dark. Several children were already examining the machine as I walked out of the store, but by this time witnessing a sale was old stuff. I didn't even wait to watch.

When I got home, Mary-Armour was waiting on the front steps.

"The New California just called," she said. "Barney says the ring machine is on the blink."

We came eventually to speak of him as Saint Barney. For although he was forced to call many a time after that to tell me that the ring machine was in need of repair, he never once showed annoyance, or threatened to disembowel me, or to throw my machines out. Some day we will erect a small statue on our front lawn, a likeness of Saint Barney O'Hara, Faithful Friend and Grocer Extraordinary.

For a while I made daily journeys to the New California Market to clear the ever-recurring jams. One day I made three trips there before noon. The jamming problem left me exhausted. It seemed to me that if a penny machine would vend bubble gum and Boston Beans months on end without a whimper, it was a damned impertinence for it to falter when it stepped up in class to nickel merchandise.

The worst part of the situation was that even when our machine was working, it did an indifferent business. My diagnosis was that the plastic cameos didn't have the appeal of the nickel-plated rings we had on order. Therefore, I was on the phone every day to Oakland, trying to hurry Mr. Murchie, the supplier I had never seen.

Murchie expected a new shipment any day now—tomorrow maybe, or the day after. But the shipment never seemed to come. I had the feeling that my order was sitting on his desk, constantly being moved to the bottom of the pile as newer orders came in. Finally I decided that the only way to get my rings was to go to Oakland in person.

Outside the Oakland office of the Murchie Specialty Company, I put on my dark glasses, pulled my hat down over my eyes, and dug my hands deep into my coat pockets, hoping to suggest the possibility of automatic pistols. Then I strode in.

"I'm Nelson from Sonoma," I growled at the 14-carat blonde behind the front desk.

I glanced furtively around the room, making sure I had a bullet for everybody. "I'm looking for my ring order," I said.

"Oh, Mr. Nelson!" the girl trilled cordially. She smiled and stood up and posed for a moment, ostensibly to let me take in her appallingly good figure. She wore a tight gray skirt and one of those fluffy, lacy blouses with a million ruffles that look so demure until you realize the whole thing is practically transparent. "We were just talking about you," she said. "Let me call Mr. Murchie." She swiveled her hips to the back door of the room and yodeled, "Esau! Here's Mr. *Nelson!*"

Esau appeared from the back room, an extravagant Aurora Borealis-type smile playing across his towhead features. He was a young man, but his face was heavily seamed with wrinkles, possibly from prolonged and over-intensive smiling. He was large, athletic, toothy, and his eyes, as he approached me, were nearly smiled shut.

"Mr. *Nelson!*" he said, crushing my hand in his grip. "How's the weather in Sonoma these days? Better than here, I'll bet!"

"It's okay," I said gruffly. "How about my rings?"

"You know," Esau said jovially, "it's a funny thing,

but we were just going to ship them out to you today. Weren't we, Julia?"

"Yes, Mr. Murchie," the girl said. She turned toward me, winked, and gave a little wriggle which set up all sorts of interesting vibrations.

"And now you can take them right along with you, if you want," Esau said.

"And save yourself all that freight!" the girl added musically.

"I hope we haven't inconvenienced you, Mr. Nelson," Esau said. "You see, up to now, we haven't been able to get enough rings together to fill an order the size of yours." He laughed. "We never expected this thing to go over so big."

"Have a chair, Mr. Nelson," the girl said.

"I have to run," Esau said, "but Miss Trelawney here will take good care of you." Still smiling, he disappeared into the back room again.

"Your rings will be here in a jiffy," said Miss Trelawney. "Would you like to look at the morning paper while you're waiting?"

I sat down, and she bent halfway over me to hand me a copy of the *Examiner*, folded open to the comic page. Her perfume, a rare blend of gardenias and attar of Dentyne, nearly asphyxiated me.

I relaxed my grip on my imaginary pistols. I sighed. I picked up the comics.

Shortly thereafter I dashed home laden with two thousand of the nickel-and-Lucite rings, plus two thousand marbles. For two dollars a thousand more I could have bought the rings already loaded with marbles, but I figured that Mary-Armour and I had more time than money and could do our own loading.

The marbles fitted the metal rings much better than they had the plastic, and fortunately we didn't have to tape them in. Nevertheless, it still took a lot of time to load. Every day or so we got a few more globefuls loaded, a few more machines converted and out on location.

The new rings were a hot item, even hotter than we had hoped, and the only problem was the incessant jamming of the machines. Machines that had been accustomed to gross four or five dollars a month when they were dispensing penny merchandise began turning in grosses of sixteen to twenty-five dollars a month—an immense sum in our economic cosmos. In Healdsburg, a ring machine proved so successful and at the same time, so erratic, that each week I had to leave the storekeeper a box full of loose rings with which to reward customers who put in a nickel and got goose-egged.

This happened to be the only ring machine in Healdsburg at the time, and the proprietor reported that kids were coming to his store from all over town. Bicycles jammed the front sidewalk of his store, and one child was chauffeur-driven thirty-two miles on two seperate occasions just to play the fabulous ring-for-a-nickel machine.

The rings cost us about two cents and brought in a nickel. The storekeeper got one cent of this, and we got the rest. Some of our tiny customers, however, were better businessmen than we. They would purchase ten rings at the Healdsburg store for five cents apiece, and then return to their grade school where, in the early days at least, the rings could be retailed at prices up to a quarter apiece.

One night, over that most useful piece of household furniture, the kitchen table, the Chairman of the Board and I were discussing the future of the nickel ring. Our hands were not idle; as usual, we were loading marbles into rings.

"There'll come a day," I said, "when every single, solitary kid in this part of the country will have more rings than he can wear."

"We hope," Mary-Armour said.

"It's a fact, the rings can't last forever," I said. "We've

got to figure out what our next move will be, after the rings go dead."

"We'll just put some other little trinket in the machines," Mary-Armour said.

"Exactly. And *I* can tell you precisely what it's going to be."

"Okay. What?"

"Yo-yos. Tiny little yo-yos."

"I don't know whether to take you seriously or not," Mary-Armour said.

"I'm dead serious," I said. "Listen, I was talking to old man Cobwell today—you know, over in Petaluma. He's got one of those new ring machines, and he was talking with the operator. You know what the operator told him? He said when rings went dead, he had a big batch of midget yo-yos he was going to spring. Now, does that give you any ideas?"

"Only that we should spring them first."

"Right! They beat us to the punch with the rings, but we're going to beat the pants off them with the yo-yos. I'm going to call Murchie in the morning and cancel our outstanding ring orders and order yo-yos instead."

Like the rings, the yo-yos were slow in coming. But this time I felt the delay was genuine, because Murchie assured me that hardly a soul had ordered yo-yos yet; the rings were still too hot an item.

And then one day the yo-yos finally arrived. Mary-Armour and I sighed with relief as we tore open the box.

Mary-Armour grabbed one. "Look!" she said, jerking her hand up and down. "They work!"

"Quit horsing around and get a clean globe," I said.

Mary-Armour dashed off to the storeroom, got a globe, and dashed back. I lifted the huge carton of yo-yos and poured the globe full.

"Blessings on them," Mary-Armour sighed. "They don't have to be loaded with marbles."

"Or Scotch-taped," I added.

I rushed our first load of yo-yos to the New California, which because of Saint Barney's unlimited patience, was our chief testing point for all kinds of experiments.

"Barney," I said to him, holding the loaded globe behind my back, "the nickel rings have done okay, haven't they?"

"They've done very nicely," Barney said. "I was surprised."

"Barney," I said, bringing the yo-yos into view, "you ain't seen nothin' yet!"

"So what's in the globe?" Barney asked.

"Yo-yos," I said. "Here, take one home to the kid. On the house. And after I put this thing on your machine, stand back for the flood of nickels!"

I spent the rest of the day on the road, replacing ring loads with yo-yo loads. By six o'clock that evening, I had half of our yo-yo inventory out on location. I didn't replace all the ring loads, of course, because we had to use up our remaining ring inventory somehow, and rings were still doing a good business.

I made one trip each day to the New California Market to give us a sort of barometric reading on how the yo-yo sales were going. And in a remarkably short time I discovered that they weren't going at all. Nobody, but nobody, wanted yo-yos.

Hindsight set in immediately.

"Naturally they don't want them!" I told Mary-Armour. "The little kids can't work 'em, for one thing, and for the big kids who can, one's plenty."

"They're surely not like the rings," Mary-Armour agreed, shaking her head.

"We didn't use our heads," I said. "We just let ourselves be stampeded into it, because some competitor said *he* was going to sell them. Well, we've got to find another item and really *think* about it this time."

The stamp-pad ring turned out to be the item. We didn't see how it could miss. Of course, it was expensive—$21.50 a thousand against $18.00 for the cabochon rings—but it was worth the difference. It was a two-tone plastic job, the face of which bore one of a number of legends in raised, backward type, such as "Kiss Me Quick," "Be My Pal," and "Jet Pilot." All you had to do was ink it, and you were ready to deface anything.

There was only one drawback. It came in four separate parts that had to be assembled. One part was the ring itself; the other three were a cylinder that fitted into the ring in place of a marble; a cap for the cylinder, turning it into a closed container; and a piece of felt to go inside the cylinder for inking purposes.

Mary-Armour and I spent hours loading our first globeful. It was an aggravating kind of work, especially since the stamp-pad rings wouldn't hold together any better than our first glow-in-the-dark rings. As a final humiliation, therefore, we had to cut strips of Scotch tape and girdle each ring.

There is nothing that will give you second thoughts about the part-time nature of a business faster than having to work at it day and night, seven days a week. Daytimes I was out on the road, unjamming nickel machines, servicing penny machines, and trying to dig up new locations. Evenings, Saturdays, and Sundays, I was seated at the kitchen table with my faithful helpmeet, loading rings, attempting to convert machines, and worrying.

For would-be businessmen, we were getting a mighty small return on the capital and effort we were putting into our venture.

And for would-be dabblers in the arts, we were getting mighty little dabbling done.

13

Machines jammed, merchants grumbled, and stamp-pad rings did so-so. Mary-Armour and I invested in a bottle of local sherry and gave the whole gumball business some deep thought.

"You know, sweetie," I said, as the rich amber liquid gurgled out of the bottle into a waiting glass on the kitchen table, "we were really dopes, weren't we? We really got good and stung."

"On the stamp-pad rings?"

"On everything. Machines, merchandise, stamp-pad rings, everything."

"Oh well," Mary-Armour said, "it's a short life but a gay one."

I took a big swig of sherry and gagged. For two dollars a gallon, what could I expect?

"Remember Tony Barloff?" Mary-Armour said. "And some of the others like him?"

"The coffee-machine guy?"

"That's right. Whenever I start feeling that we got stung, I like to think of those people. It makes me realize that we *could* have got stung a lot worse."

In a way, I had to admit that Mary-Armour was right. Compared with some of the characters who inhabited the blue-sky fringes of the vending-machine world, the No-Name gentlemen who relieved us of our bankbook were paragons of probity. They were like General Motors stock as compared with those worthless shares your Uncle Harry used to wallpaper his rumpus room. Therefore, instead of vacuuming our wallet and giving us no machines in return, as a real post-office-wall con man would have done, our No-Name friends had vacuumed it and given us a hundred overpriced machines, mostly on stands, mostly in locations of dubious merit.

Our realization of the fact that we could be worse off, though not much, was heightened every now and then when we ran into someone like Geordie Swansdown. Geordie dropped by one hot Tuesday afternoon. He came, like most of our entrepreneurial experiences, through a newspaper ad. It had read: "Something new in vending. Virgin field. Write ARH, 25 Glandis Avenue, Vallejo."

I figured that if something new in vending was coming to Sonoma County, I ought to know about it. So I dropped ARH a post card, inquiring what product his machines dispensed.

By return mail I received a carefully worded reply in which Arthur R. Hodgkins explained that the exotic nature of his product made a written description of it very drab indeed. It had to be seen to be believed. Therefore, with my kind permission, and with absolutely no obligation to me, of course, he would drop by in the near future to demonstrate what he had to offer.

A week later, Geordie Swansdown phoned. Mr. Hodgkins, Swansdown said, regretted extremely that he would not have the pleasure of calling on me, as he had suddenly been called out of the city for an indefinite period. (I wondered if it might be five to ten, with time off for good behavior.) Nevertheless, he, Swansdown, would be delighted to drop by at my convenience and demonstrate how his machines would profitably strip this virgin field of its virginity.

"What's the product?" I asked.

"Mr. Nelson," said Swansdown, "it's just too complex to explain over the phone. When may I show it to you?"

I set a date a couple of days away and waited. On the appointed day Swansdown telephoned fifteen minutes before he was to arrive, to say that he would be half an hour late. Two hours later he arrived at the wheel of a big, black Buick.

Swansdown, as he stepped from his conservative automobile, was the apotheosis of city slickers. He wore a pearl-gray homburg, a pearl-gray double-breasted suit, and a courtly pearl-gray smile. His socks, tie, and breastpocket handkerchief were all a uniform fluorescent maroon. His shoes were narrow, pointed, and yellow. He was carefully barbered, and his tiny gray mustache looked as though it had been clipped only minutes before.

Mary-Armour and I introduced ourselves. "Geordie Swansdown," he said, bowing low from the hips. "It's a gen-u-wine pleasure."

I realized that Swansdown was probably more accustomed to working in living rooms, but since it was a bright sunshiny day, I asked him to set up his roadshow around our outdoor barbecue table.

"Gladly, gladly," he smiled. He took a long look around our acreage, as though appraising it, and drew in a deep, satisfied breath. For all he knew, we owned the place.

From the back seat of his car he removed a big imitation leather box and a large loose-leaf notebook. He laid them in the middle of the sun-drenched table. He then carefully removed his coat, and after flicking a few invisible specks of dust from one sleeve, hung it over the back of a chair. He adjusted his flowered elastic armbands in the manner of a man about to operate the shell game, presumably to show us that he had nothing up his sleeves, and sat down. At no time did he remove the pearl-gray homburg.

After courteously requesting that Mary-Armour sit on one side of him, and I on the other, Swansdown flipped his notebook open to the first page. It revealed a lavishly printed piece of stationery, a two-color job showing a Forty-Niner panning gold in the middle of the lush letterhead. On it was typed this businesslike proclamation:

"To whom it may concern: This is to certify that Geordie Swansdown is an officially authorized representative of Pacific Mechanical Merchandisers, Inc. As such, he is empowered to negotiate contracts, accept money, detail routes, and perform such other services as may be necessary or desirable in promoting the interests of the customers of Pacific Mechanical Merchandisers, Inc."

The proclamation ran on for four or five more paragraphs. It discussed the well-attested reliability of Mr. Swansdown and his long years of experience in the coin-machine field. At the bottom of the page it was signed by "R. Winterrich, Pres." I happened to catch a look at the signature date and found that the paper had been signed three days previously.

Swansdown flipped the page. Here was another proclamation, much like the first but directed this time to all bank presidents and finance company executives. It restated Swansdown's official connection with Pacific Mechanical Merchandisers, and said that the home office would appreciate any help that could be given to Geordie in financing the sale of vending machines.

"I sometimes get pretty far from home base," Geordie

said in explanation, "and this helps me to get financing for people."

The date on the second document was the same as the first. That hardly gave Geordie time to get much farther from home base than Sonoma County.

"How long have you worked for Pacific?" I asked.

"Oh, not too long," he said. "Only a few months, really. I used to work for an outfit in Frisco, but I didn't like the way they did business. So when this opportunity came to go to work for Winterrich, I jumped at it. The boss is a great old guy," he added, chuckling appreciatively. "We all love working for him."

"What ever happened to Mr. Hodgkins?" I asked.

"What's that?"

"Mr. Hodgkins."

"Oh . . . Hodgkins. Well, Hodgkins is on another assignment. He got called away."

Swansdown turned another page. "Did you know," he said, "that more than *blank* million dollars worth of merchandise was sold through vending machines last year?" He paused, as if waiting for someone to say "Gee whiz!" Mary-Armour and I remained silent. Swansdown drew in a breath and continued.

"That's nothing," he said. "It's getting bigger every minute. Here's a page from *Vend* magazine which shows that it will probably increase more than *blank* per cent next year!"

He cocked his head on one side and looked significantly at Mary-Armour, then at me. We said nothing.

Swansdown flipped the page to a reprint of a feature article on vending from a Chicago newspaper. " 'A new type of retail outlet,' " he read, " 'the vending machine, is burgeoning . . .' "

"Excuse me, Mr. Swansdown," I broke in. "Our time is limited, and I'm sure yours is, too. I wonder if we could talk about your particular deal."

Swansdown looked hurt. He enjoyed staging his little show. Nevertheless he agreed. "Okay," he said. He started to flip the page. "Wait! Here's a *good* one—it's an article from *Nation's Business* . . ."

"If you please, Mr. Swansdown," I interrupted, "we already know a little about the background of the coin-machine business. But we don't know what you are selling."

The faintest glimmer of a frown crossed Swansdown's brow. It was obvious that he felt cheated. He was proud of the fine presentation he had prepared. It had taken plenty of trouble to assemble all that material and insert it in the glassine pages of his notebook, and *by God, he was going to read it!*

Unless . . . well, he knew he had to humor his prospects, no matter how much it hurt.

Forcing a smile, Swansdown flipped quickly through the rest of his book, scanning each page briefly, moving his lips and muttering phrases which identified that part of the presentation. It was as though skipping a page might break the train of thought necessary to bring one of his big deals to a successful conclusion.

"Outlook for vending—" he said, running his finger down a page—"vending in industry . . . in schools . . . vending candy, cigarettes . . . nylons . . . Say! Did you know they're even vending nylons through machines these days? Oh, yes," he continued quickly, when he got no response, "we'll get on . . . vending vitamin pills . . . personal comfort products . . ." He scanned a few more pages and shut the book reluctantly.

"Now," he said, shooting his cuffs, "I'll show you what I've got." He opened the cover of his black box about an inch.

"This is absolutely terrific!" he said, his enthusiasm beginning to mount again. "There's nothing like it. It's brand-new. It was tested first in Ohio, and was a terrific sensation. We've already put a few machines out here in California, and they're making money hand over fist. Yes, sir, *hand . . . over . . . fist!*"

He opened the box another inch. "Now, this particular merchandise appeals to children. And if you don't think the kids have the money these days, you're dead wrong, brother, dead wrong. The kids of today have plenty of money. And this . . . is . . . what . . . they're . . . spending it . . . for!"

With each word he jerked the case open a smidgen further, until finally it was open all the way, dramatically revealing two machines filled with the same kind of cabochon rings of which we had 1,300 resting not fifty feet away.

"This," Swansdown said, his voice vibrant with emotion, "is the biggest deal in vending today!" He sat back triumphantly, perspiration streaming down his face, while Mary-Armour and I examined the machines wordlessly for about a minute.

"Is that all they vend—rings?" I asked.

"These machines will vend *anything!*" Swansdown replied.

Mary-Armour looked him straight in the eye.

"Nylons?" she said.

"Well, no, not nylons," Swansdown said, frowning slightly. "I mean anything of the general size and shape of these rings."

"You can't just keep on selling rings indefinitely, can you?" I asked.

"Aha!" said Swansdown, his gray eyes lighting brightly. His face looked definitely Mephistophelean, and I began to have an inkling of why he never removed his hat. "We've got that one all figured out. If the rings ever go sour, we're going to spring a brand-new one on them. Look," he said, pulling a tiny object from his pocket. "Yo-yos!"

Swansdown held the yo-yo out for inspection. "Isn't that amazing?" he asked.

Mary-Armour took the yo-yo and worked it up and down casually. "It certainly is," she said.

"Say, you're pretty good with that thing," Swansdown said. Mary-Armour smiled a gracious thank-you and handed the yo-yo back.

"And when *that* goes dead," Swansdown said, "look!" He reached into the side pocket of his neatly hung-up coat and produced two or three stamp-pad rings.

"Each one says something different," he said, squinting at one in the sunlight. "This one says 'Kiss Me Quick,' I think. Here, you look at it."

"It says 'Be My Pal,' " I said. "I guess that's about the same thing."

Swansdown broke into loud, insincere guffaws. "Haw, haw," he said. "That's a good one."

"How much do these machines cost, Mr. Swansdown?" I asked.

"In just a moment I will tell you," he said. "But first let's look at the profit picture."

Swansdown opened his notebook to a page with a rather complicated grid. It purported to show, in the same way that the newspaper advertisements frequently did, how much one might expect to earn from a given number of machines, devoting a certain number of hours a week to tending them. I invite the reader to remember at this time that we were divinely happy whenever a bulk machine emptied once a month. Swansdown's grid was worked out for excellent, good, and fair locations—that is, for machines that emptied once every three days, once every six days, and once every ten days.

"I've even seen these machines empty in as little as three hours!" he said. "With my own eyes. But that *is* a little unusual," he conceded sportingly. "Now. Suppose you had ten machines, and they emptied every three days. The merchandise in each machine costs you eight dollars and brings back twenty-five dollars. You pay twenty per cent or five dollars to the location, and that leaves you twelve dollars. Emptying every three days—twice a week, let's say—that's a net profit to you of twenty-four dollars a machine, or two hundred and forty dollars a week for only ten machines!"

"But," he continued, with the air of a man who is not trying to high-pressure anyone, "let's be conservative. Let's suppose they empty not once every three days, not even once a week, but *only once every ten days!* That's three times a month, right? Even at that slow rate you've still got a net profit of three hundred and sixty dollars a month!"

Neither Mary-Armour nor I could think of anything suitable to say.

"Okay," said Swansdown, "now about the cost. Loaded and on location a machine like this will cost you $67.50. This other machine, which is slightly more durable and can be converted to sell for a nickel, a dime, or a penny, would cost you $78.50."

"On location and filled?"

"That is correct, sir."

I raised my eyebrows and looked thoughtful.

"Now," Swansdown continued. "How we place them. Pacific Mechanical Merchandisers keeps a large staff of men on the road, collecting slips like these." He flashed a printed form labeled "Vending Machine Authorization Slip." It was intended to be signed by a storekeeper, and the burden of the copy was that the storekeeper was faint with desire at the thought of having one of Swansdown's machines installed in his store.

"We go out and get these slips," said Geordie, "and when we've collected enough of them in any given locality, we advertise and try to find a man who is capable of taking the route over. Naturally we try to pick the best man for the job. Now, I've already interviewed several people, and frankly, if you don't mind my saying so, you're head and shoulders above them all. If you're interested, I think

I could swing the deal your way without any further ado."

"That's terribly nice of Mr. Swansdown, isn't it?" Mary-Armour said. "But don't you think we ought to talk it over, Jim?"

"I suppose we should," I said. "After all, it's a lot of money."

"Not so much," Swansdown interjected coolly, "when you think of what it's going to bring in. Why, it would pay itself off in a couple of months!"

"That's true," I said, "but we've got a couple of other profitable deals cooking too. We'll have to weigh this one against them."

Swansdown was perspiring heavily as he packed his machines back into his Buick and prepared to leave. Mary-Armour offered him a glass of water. He gulped it, crooking his little finger elegantly.

"By the way," Swansdown said, as he handed the glass back and got into his car, "what kind of work do you do, Mr. Nelson?"

"I'm a professional pigeon-breeder," I said.

The suggestion of a frown crossed Swansdown's face. Then he brightened and winked at Mary-Armour.

"You must make a pretty good thing out of it," he said, "to have a place like this."

"Oh, we make ends meet," I said casually.

Swansdown thought it was modesty, and I knew it was a lie.

14

The Business Opportunities columns of the local newspapers continued to bubble over with big deals. It seemed as though every promoter in the country had decided to come to Sonoma County and sell vending-machine routes that would compete with the slowly sinking Nelsons.

Hot on the heels of Geordie Swansdown's virgin-field ad came one in which the promoter stated that he was looking for "a man capable of earning $12,000 to $15,000 a year." Naturally, only the smallest of investments was required. "You will be sponsored by a local civic organization," the ad continued, adding that the products to be vended included Dentyne, Wrigley's, and other items that we handled in our tab-gum venders.

The ad had instant success, for I suddenly began to notice new tab-gum venders quite similar to ours popping up at various places in the town where the ad had appeared. Each one bore a decalcomania stating that a portion of the proceeds from the machine was being donated to the local Lions Club for its youth activities fund.

Now, the so-called "sponsored route" has a lot of advantages over the ordinary unsponsored one we were operating. Its chief virtue, perhaps, is the fact that the Lions Club, or whatever organization is doing the sponsoring, actually does get money from the machines to carry on its charitable work. Thus, once the sponsoring club has helped to build the route, it can sit back and reap a percentage of the gross sales for as long as the route stays in business— and all without spending a penny of its own money.

The sponsor, of course, in this sort of route, does most of the location getting. Here's roughly how it works: Harry Bufnik, a genial Lion whose wife runs up a big monthly tab at the Grobnitz Supermarket, gets Joe Grobnitz on the phone one morning.

"Joe?" Bufnik says. "Harry Bufnik."

"Good morning, Mr. Bufnik," says Grobnitz.

"Mrs. Bufnik been in there yet this morning, Joe?"

"Not yet, Mr. Bufnik," says Grobnitz. "You want I should tell her to call you?"

"No, Joe," says Bufnik, "I just wondered. She has the check, I believe, for last month's bill, that's all. Quite a piece of change, too, you old robber! No, I called about something else, Joe."

"Yes, Mr. Bufnik?"

Bufnik then cuts grocer Grobnitz in on the information that the Lions are sponsoring a charitable deal, all for the youth activities fund, and he's sure Joe would like to have one of the machines in his store, eh? Just to show his heart's in the right place?

Joe, an experienced storekeeper who already shelters a Kiwanis gumball machine, knows that a small percentage of the new machine's sales will be paid to the Lions Club, and the rest will go to the man who owns and operates the machine. Grobnitz will not get a penny out of the deal. The machine will only be in the way. But then Grobnitz thinks briefly about the $150 that Bufnik's wife spends in his store each month. He grits his teeth and smiles into the phone. Naturally, he says, he is willing to do anything for the youth of the town; nothing is too good for them.

"I knew you'd see it that way, Joe," Bufnik says.

Bufnik then calls the promoter and tells him to put a machine in the Grobnitz store, which the promoter does, and it is then turned over to the local operator who has sold his shoe-repair shop and is investing the proceeds in a gum route.

If you contend that my rendition of this operation sounds a little sour-grape-like, I will agree wholeheartedly. As the operator of an unsponsored route at the time these machines came into "my" territory, I was on the outside looking in, and my grapes were pure alum. The sponsored operator, I knew, was paying only a 10 per cent commission to the Lions Club, while my commissions—often in the same store—ranged up to 25 per cent. As long as the sponsored operator didn't actually kick the storekeeper's shins, he would remain *persona grata,* thanks to the grocer's humanitarian desire to aid youth.

The only way I could bring comparable pressure on a merchant would be to surprise him kissing a female clerk in the back storeroom.

Every day or so I saw more Lions machines pop up on location. And all the while the come-on ad kept beseeching men capable of earning $15,000 a year to gather 'round.

At the sight of each new machine, an icicle jabbed into my heart. Each Lions Club location represented just one more spot that was closed to my sporadic relocating efforts.

I answered the ad myself, by post card, just to find out what kind of deal it was. A day or so later I got a phone call from a man named Ivor Marvelin "with Innerna-shional Amalgamated outa Chicago." While Marvelin spieled out the facts I wanted to know—prices, commissions, etc.—I began to imagine the heights Geordie Swansdown might have reached, had he been operating under the sheltering umbrella of the Lions Club!

The following day I got my big idea: If I couldn't lick 'em, I'd join 'em! Hurriedly I called the president of the Lions Club to see if he didn't want to sponsor me along with his other operators. I was going to explain how this would benefit us both—the Lions would get additional revenue from my machines, and in return I could use the prestige of the Lions to get some good new locations that might otherwise be unapproachable.

The prexy's secretary came on the wire. "Just a moment, please," she said.

While I waited, I heard a man—presumably the prexy himself—telling someone else that the club was planning to put out 150 machines in the town. One hundred and fifty machines! This, I figured with sinking heart, would freeze my tab-gum venders dead in their tracks.

The club president was courteous and thoughtful about my suggestion, but I hung up feeling that nothing would come of it. Well, I decided, the Lions Club wasn't the only organization that could sponsor gum machines!

Immediately I called on the head of the Rotary Club and stated graciously that in return for Rotary sponsorship, I would gladly turn a generous percentage of my gross over to the club. But the Rotary, I was informed brusquely, wanted nothing to do with vending machines or with me. I phoned the head of Kiwanis, who was courteous but doubtful, since the club already had ball-gum venders in its program. I tried to spoor the head of the Boy Scouts to his lair to see if his organization didn't want to benefit from my services, but unfortunately I could never find the head man in his lean-to.

Suicide excepted, there was only one course left open to me. That was to intensify my relocating campaign so that I could land as many new locations as possible before the flood of Lions Club machines swept over my head. I spent the next twelve weekdays on the road, introducing myself, demonstrating my machines, urging and cajoling, trying to upgrade our route. My old friend, the law of averages, saw to it that I got a few new locations, but they really weren't much better than the places I'd pulled the machines out of. Every day I expected the great inundation of Lions Club machines.

But somehow, the flood never came. Within a couple of weeks the number of Lions Club machines seemed to stabilize—possibly because there weren't enough "men capable of earning $12,000 to $15,000" running around loose. Realizing this, I drew my first deep breath in more than a month and thanked my lucky stars that, with a couple of minor exceptions, the affairs of the Multivend Company were in about the same shape as before Ivor Marvelin invaded the territory.

At the request of a supermarket operator I bought a second-hand stamp machine and installed it. I sold eight cents' worth of U.S. postage for a dime. I had been told (by Skillman, from whom I bought the machine—once a pigeon, always a pigeon, I guess) that a stamp machine in a moderately good location might easily gross forty dollars a month. Of this sum, of course, eight dollars would be my profit.

The idea was so appealing that, without waiting to see how the first machine did, I bought a second one. I installed it in a brand-new supermarket, partly for the eight dollars of pure profit it would bring me, and partly because I thought that installing it in this particular market might lead to the installation of other machines in the same store.

Between them, the two machines barely grossed ten

dollars a month. I relocated them immediately—in a couple of small, out-of-the-way groceries—and managed to bring the monthly total up to twenty-five dollars.

Even if the machines didn't add much to our income, they did provide the knowledge that people almost never put a slug in a stamp machine. Somehow they seem to connect the purchase of stamps with the U.S. government, and feel that slugging a stamp vender would be the equivalent of robbing the mails.

At the plywood mill, meanwhile, vending was having its problems. My own machines were operating nobly, but the candy-bar machine, operated by someone else, was becoming notorious.

"When you gonna fill that one up?" a plywood worker asked me one morning, pointing to the candy-bar machine.

"It's not my machine," I explained.

"The gaw-dam thing!" he exclaimed. "It never has no gaw-dam candy in it!"

"And when it does, it don't come out," another man chimed in.

I raised my eyebrows and tried to look as innocent as possible.

"I put three nickels in that bastard last night," said a third man indignantly, "and all I git was a horselaugh!"

This fickle attitude of the candy machine soon resulted in its demolition by an overemotional worker who felt that, after fruitlessly inserting seven consecutive nickels, he deserved, at the very least, exercise.

The following day the irate operator yanked the remains of his machine out of the plant, leaving in its place two notes, one an angry scribble to the villain who had smashed the machine, promising vengeance, the other a honeyed *billet-doux* to the nonguilty members of the night shift, asking them to squeal on the smasher.

I waited a decent period after the demise of the candy-bar machine (about thirty minutes), and then installed a bulk machine to vend a handful of mixed nuts for a nickel. Thanks to the candy-bar machine's absence, the nut machine was an instant and overwhelming success.

On my first trip to service the nut machine, I was subjected to a fierce cross-examination. I arrived in the middle of the day shift's lunch hour.

"Here comes the robber!" someone shouted as I walked in. I wondered briefly if my machine might not soon go the way of the candy-bar dispenser. "Got your gun with you?"

"Good morning, gentlemen," I said, batting my eyes and smiling.

"Hey, buddy, how many these here nuts you supposed to get for a nickel?"

"Oh, about eight to twelve," I answered. "It varies."

"Well, I got gypped. It only give me seven."

"You're lucky, Dutch," said another. "It's only supposed to give out six. When it gives seven, there's this hand reaches outa the machine and takes one back."

"Oh, it's not as bad as all that, is it?" I said.

"Yeah, it is," Dutch said. "You got any free samples?"

"Sure," I said. "They're in the machine. All you need to get one is a nickel."

This got a laugh from everyone except Dutch.

"So we got a wise guy on our hands now," Dutch said. "Hey, when you gonna skip all this crud and put in an honest-to-God candy-bar machine?"

"Who?" I said. "Me?"

"No, I mean your great-aunt Minnie's illegitimate stepsister!" Dutch said.

There were several reasons why I didn't want to put in a candy-bar machine. For one thing, the sight of the mangled body of the last machine was still green in my memory. For another, a new machine would cost nearly two hundred dollars, and two hundred dollars taken from our savings account and spent on equipment—unless it

229

produced like crazy—would bring us about forty-five days nearer the end of our rope.

Besides, the nickel nuts, in the absence of the candy-bar machine, were selling amazingly well, and the profit margin on bulk nuts was considerably better than on candy bars.

"I still think we ought to do it," Mary-Armour said, when I discussed it with her.

"Why? The nuts are going like mad."

"Suppose some other candy-bar operator comes along and puts a machine in. What will happen to the nut trade then?"

"You've got a point," I said.

"Why don't you take a look around in San Francisco to see if you can find a used machine," Mary-Armour said.

No-Name, of course, had just the thing. It was a beat-up old machine with a cracked mirror on the front, but it worked, and it only cost sixty dollars. I bought it, installed it, stocked it, and stood back hopefully.

The first month it grossed eighty dollars. As soon as I saw how well it was going, I dashed right into San Francisco, bought another second-hand machine from No-Name, and installed it in the other plywood mill.

The addition of these two machines increased the net earnings of the Multivend Company by about forty-five dollars a month. This was a real shot in the arm. And then one evening the boys on the night shift at the number-one mill discovered that a penny worked our ancient machine just as efficiently as a dime. Within a few hours the machine was completely empty, and the shift foreman was on the phone, asking if I would come and refill it.

There was great merriment among the members of the night shift when I emptied the coin box on the table to count the take and discovered it was full of copper cents.

"That machine gives real value!" one of them screamed

in my ear over the others' gales of laughter. "The biggest penny candy bar in town!"

A small soldering job soon got this machine back on a diet of dimes, and the two candy-bar machines provided a tiny pinpoint of light in an otherwise dismal landscape.

By now most of the nickel charm machines had slowed to a walk, and the rest to a crawl. Many of them were grossing less than when they'd carried penny merchandise. They jammed about every second play, and a number of storekeepers were becoming so irate at having to keep track of refunded nickels that they began to threaten to throw the machines out. Only good, dear, kind, sweet Saint Barney O'Hara still smiled and said hello when I walked into his store to clear a jam. The others merely snarled.

Therefore, with great reluctance I began converting the charm machines back to penny operation, undoing all that I had done. It was a sad process, and it made me feel a great deal older, but to tell the truth, not much wiser.

The route now consisted of forty-nine tab-gum venders (one had been stolen), fifty-seven bulk venders (I had picked up seven used machines from a grounded pigeon for five dollars apiece), two stamp machines, and the two candy-bar machines. In December we grossed $633.38. After paying commissions and merchandise costs, we had $249.51 left.

"Two-forty-nine, fifty-one," I said to Mary-Armour as I laid down my pencil. We were sitting at the big kitchen table, sipping steamy black coffee. It was nine o'clock in the evening, and the giant oaks outside the window were waving spastically in the cold winter wind. "Of course, we've got to pay the usual taxes and gas and everything. But it's still the best we've ever done."

"That's terrific, sweetie," Mary-Armour said. She leaned her elbows on the table and cradled her head in her hands.

Her blue eyes looked shiny and beautiful. "You've done a wonderful job," she said.

"You, too," I said. "You've been in on everything—all the decisions. And you've loaded a million globes."

"I haven't done anything. You're the one who goes out on the road."

"Who got that big supermarket location in Sonoma?" I asked. "Three machines."

"Oh, that," Mary-Armour said offhandedly. She leaned back and ran her hands through her blond hair. "I just happened to be talking to the manager . . ."

"I know," I said. "You just happened to talk him into a big deal." I looked back at the column of figures I'd just added up. "Two-forty-nine. That's really okay, isn't it?"

"It's sensational."

"It's our best month so far."

"Yes, it is. It's really a record."

"Of course, we can't *live* on two-forty-nine, fifty-one," I said.

"No, we can't . . . but it's still a fine showing."

"Oh, it's a fine showing, all right," I said. "There's no doubt about that. I just wish we didn't have to take a hundred bucks—or two hundred or three hundred every month to make up the rest of our living expenses."

"Me, too."

"We haven't got too many months' worth of living left in that account," I said.

"I know it."

Mary-Armour got the coffeepot from the stove and replenished our cups. When she sat down again, we lifted our cups in the air and clinked them together.

"Well, here's to the record," I said.

"Yes, we certainly did well," Mary-Armour said. "And we'll do even better next month!"

"Sure we will," I said. *"Excelsior!"*

"Excelsior it is!"

We sat in silence for a few moments, inhaling the pungent aroma of the coffee and staring at one another over the rims of our cups. Outside, the wind was whipping the trees mercilessly.

"Let's sell the damned route," I said.

"Yes," Mary-Armour said. "Let's."

15

"For sale: Established, profitable vending route . . ."
We ran our ad for a week in the Santa Rosa newspaper,
quoting a set of seductive dollar figures labeled, "monthly
net after paying commissions and merchandise costs."
During the preceding four months, the ad pointed out, this
figure had varied between $212 and $250.

This bait lured exactly fifteen unwary prospects into our
living room, where they were subjected to all sorts of
allurements, the chief one being my rose-tinted travelogue
on the bucolic joys of gumballing.

"You should have lunch some time," my standard spiel
ran, "under those leafy giants that border sparkling little
Maacama Creek. It's really pleasant, you know, just sitting
there in the warm sun with a couple of toothsome sandwiches and a copy of————." (Proust, Mickey Spillane, or
Bugs Bunny, whichever seemed applicable.)

Practice makes perfect, of course, and after a while my rendition of these bosky delights reached such soaring heights that Mary-Armour, who ordinarily ducked out of sight when a prospect appeared, actually went out of her way to be present during this part of my pitch. She said it made her feel like crying to hear how beautiful life could be if a person were only in the gumball racket.

The aim of these pastoral elegies, of course, was to put the prospect in such a good frame of mind that he wouldn't mind hearing that the so-called "monthly net" figure took no account whatever of auto expense, sales taxes, license fees, etc. We hated to reveal this sordid news, but we revealed it anyhow, to each and every one of them. Much as we longed to high-pressure our clientele after the florid style of Geordie Swansdown, we never departed from the true facts of the matter.

Out of the fifteen replies to our initial seven-day ad, the first thirteen people were just looking, thank you. They had in mind spending something between $200 and $500 and using the easy-pay plan. Our asking price was $4,900, about $700 less than we had tied up in the business, but we were ready to make sizable concessions.

Prospect number fourteen, a Mr. Iceland, came by with his wife one Sunday evening. We talked vending for nearly two hours. It sounded like a pretty good deal to him, and the price didn't seem to scare him. Naturally, before he committed himself, he wanted to cruise the route with me. We set the following Wednesday for the Grand Tour.

Monday and Tuesday were lovely California days, as nice as winter can be. The sun burned down on pale winter faces, and we all thought about how lucky we were not to be shoveling snow. On Wednesday morning, Mr. Iceland showed up bright and early in a driving rainstorm that lasted all day.

Iceland was a man of few words. I did manage to extract from him, however, the fact that he had recently operated an egg hatchery in the Midwest. Prior to that he had spent thirteen years in the "corn game."

"You mean farming?" I asked.

"Lord, no!" he said. "Bingo."

"Bingo?"

"We used corn kernels to cover up the numbers on the cards," he said. "Traveling carnival. I ran the Bingo game."

In an effort to give Iceland the complete picture quickly, thereby speeding up his purchase of the route, I drove him to every single location in one frenzied day. This meant we had to cover a considerable amount of territory in a hurry. I found it grueling, particularly as Iceland had no questions, few comments, and twice went to sleep sitting in the seat beside me. I bought him lunch; I staggered on with my one-man conversation; I told him all the ins and outs of the vending-machine business, and when I ran out of things to say, I told him all over again.

Iceland's parting remark, as he got out of my car in Napa, was cryptic: "Well, maybe I'll be seeing you," he said.

Mary-Armour and I both took aspirins that night and went to bed early. We felt sure we had heard the last of Iceland. But two mornings later he appeared unexpectedly at our back door and said he wanted to go out again. While I put on a necktie and tried to recover from my surprise, Mary-Armour plied Iceland with coffee and questions about hatching eggs.

Iceland and I spent another wordless day. Once again I bought him lunch, once again I explained in the minutest detail the delights of the vending-machine business. Once again at the end of the day, after discussing prices, means of financing, etc., Iceland got out of the car with another noncommittal farewell.

"See you around," he said.

We haven't seen him around since.

It wasn't hard for us to transfer our hopes to Mr. Fenwick. Mr. Fenwick was the exact opposite of Iceland. He looked like a composite of the fathers of all our most respectable friends. He dressed conservatively, came from New England, was literate, talkative, and gray-haired. In addition to these sterling qualifications, he could point back to a successful career with several distinguished companies as a mechanical engineer. Since retirement, he had built and sold several houses, partly as diversion and partly as a means of augmenting his retirement income. He wanted to know all about the vending-machine business, and as I explained it to him, he offered numerous ideas on how to improve our operation.

"Now, it would probably be wise," he said, "to have some placards printed up, saying 'Out of Order,' wouldn't it? Have it on a string so your location owner could just slip it over the machine whenever it went haywire. Right?"

"That's a terribly sound suggestion, Mr. Fenwick," I said, "although you understand, of course, that it's quite unusual for a machine to go—as you say—'haywire.' "

"Um," he said. "Incidentally, what kind of accounting system do you use—Lifo or Fifo?"

"I beg pardon?"

"Last in, first out, or first in, first out? We used Lifo, the last place I was employed."

"And where was that, Mr. Fenwick?" I inquired hastily, hoping to get the spotlight off our system of keeping books.

"General Shovel and Roadscraper," he said. "They favored Fifo for many years, but they finally had to come around to Lifo."

"Eventually," I said, "everybody does." I smiled. "Now you were asking me about merchandise sources. I get most of my supplies in San Francisco . . ."

As I spieled on, I was struck once again by how much harder it is to talk extravagantly about an actual, established route than about one that is still only a gleam in the promoter's eye. The splendid locations the silver-tongued promoter is going to get for you are invariably more glamorous and profitable than the actual meat markets, drugstores, and restaurants where an operator's machines can actually be seen in operation.

With Mr. Fenwick, however, the tangible quality of our route was a real asset. He had already talked to numerous shysters who were operating out of their hats (he had even talked to No-Name), and he had written them down as blue-sky promoters. He didn't want to buy a pig in a poke, and he considered it an advantage that he could actually go out and see and touch the machines I was telling him about.

Mr. Fenwick and I spent a day cruising the route. I was a little smarter than I had been with Iceland—I made no attempt to cover the entire route in one day. We took life easy and enjoyed our nice, sunny day. We ate sandwiches and drank milk beside a green field with wooded hills in the background. We discussed vending. We discussed engineering. We discussed Mr. Fenwick's son, his daughter, his son-in-law, his clever grandchildren, the good things in life (almost none of which, according to Mr. Fenwick, was available any more), the danger of too much government, the crushing burden of taxes. Mr. Fenwick liked to be outdoors. He liked Sonoma County. He thought it would be pleasant to do exactly what we were doing, namely to breeze around the countryside filling machines, eating sandwiches, and collecting pennies. He thought the price and down payment about right. In fact, if the house he had just finished sold soon enough, he could pay the whole amount in cash.

Mr. Fenwick was extremely eager to come with me the following day to tour the remainder of the route. Needless to say, I was a bit eager myself.

"There's only one difficulty, Mr. Nelson," he told me,

as we prepared to part company. "I may have to put my car in the shop briefly tomorrow."

He'd driven out from San Francisco in it, and it looked okay to me.

"Something's wrong with it?" I asked.

"It's the thermostat in the cooling system," he said. "It doesn't permit the engine to develop enough heat for really efficient operation."

"Runs cold, eh?"

"Precisely. You see, an internal combustion engine, to develop peak efficiency, requires that a certain amount of heat be retained in the cylinder block, and in the pistons themselves. Now in my car, the cooling system is, well, almost too efficient. It works to the detriment of the combustion unit."

"I see," I said.

"Now, I don't believe it should require any major work to rectify the matter. Merely an adjustment of the thermostat—or maybe the installation of a new one. At any rate, Mr. Nelson, I think I'd better call you from San Francisco tonight, after I've talked to my mechanic, to let you know if I'll be able to make it tomorrow."

Having grown cynical in the service of King Gumball, I recognized that this maneuver was just an elaborate way to slip out of my clutches.

"Sure," I said coolly. "You give me a call."

At seven-thirty that evening, true to his word, Mr. Fenwick did call from San Francisco. I felt ashamed that I had doubted his word.

His car, Mr. Fenwick explained, really did need attention. It had run very badly on the way back to the city. He was putting it in the shop for a day. He would telephone me no later than the following Monday to let me know when it would be possible for him to tour the remainder of the route.

239

And so, in a flurry of courtesy and polite chit-chat, the last echoes of Mr. Fenwick's voice went glimmering faintly down the moonlit telephone wires.

Well, good-by, Mr. Fenwick, wherever you are. Farewell to you and your cold-blooded automobile. Maybe the mechanics couldn't fix it after all—maybe that's why I never heard from you again. Maybe you lost my telephone number. Maybe you fell sick—I hope not. Anyhow, here's good luck to you and your chilly Studebaker and your children and your grandchildren.

16

Spring came again, almost as soon as our last prospect had vanished. Spring came with a million yellow acacias, and warm sunshine, and a litter of tiny mewing kittens under the back porch. Spring brought better spirits, and even though spring couldn't take our machines off our hands, the warm days made it easier to bite the bullet and resign ourselves to staying in the gum business a while longer.

We continued advertising the route for sale in the Santa Rosa paper, daily and Sunday. From time to time we changed the copy, adding a folksy headline such as "Need Spare-Time Dough?" or "Look at the Record!"

Prospects came, and prospects went, but no buyers.

The fruit blossoms soon disappeared, turning into tiny green replicas of mature fruit, the kittens grew larger and spent most of their time avoiding Jamie and Cleo, and the Chairman of the Board knitted furiously, trying to complete a wardrobe for a new member of the firm who was due in five weeks.

And then one morning, when the baby's due date was almost upon us, I suddenly lost my appetite, picked up a low fever, and began to complain of a stiff neck. Two days later I was in the hospital with bulbar polio.

Right here and now I wish to state that I am one of the luckier persons on this earth, for my case of polio was a relatively light one. I don't mean that my stay in the hospital was just a gay holiday, pinching nurses and all that, but rather that I never reached the iron-lung stage or developed any of those unhappy complications where they have to cut a hole in your throat and insert a tube so you can breathe.

The county hospital in Santa Rosa had the only nearby facilities for isolation, so I took up residence in a ward there, felt awful, got excellent care, and spent a great deal of time worrying. I worried about Mary-Armour and the impending blessed event, I worried about myself, I worried about our finances and the gumball route.

Mary-Armour came to the hospital every day, even though the authorities wouldn't let her come in. She discovered where my window was, and found that by taking off her shoes and walking barefoot through a bit of artistic landscaping, she could get close enough for me to hear her voice. She told me that everything was humming along nicely at home, that she was fine, that Jamie was fine, and not to worry about a thing.

Days passed, and days, and more days. Time seemed to stretch on endlessly. Finally I was declared noncontagious, and was moved to a room in another hospital, the same hospital where our baby, who was now three weeks over due, would be born.

"The baby and I are waiting till you get out of the

hospital," Mary-Armour told me one afternoon as she entered my room for her daily visit.

"Listen, chum," I said, "don't be so polite. You go ahead and have the baby, and we'll all be here together."

"Except Jamie," she said. "We'll have to think of a way to work him in."

"He can have his tonsils out," I said.

"Fine," Mary-Armour said. "By the way, I've got some good news."

"Shoot," I said. "I love good news."

"I dug into our polio policy and our health insurance policy, and they'll both pay off. While you're here, you not only have all your medical expenses taken care of, but on top of it you're making $100-a-week!"

"*I am?*"

I lay back against the crisp pillow, feeling faint. At last I'd achieved the ideal I'd aimed at a year and a half before: $100-a-week, and no work.

"That's not all, either," Mary-Armour said. "I've dug up a couple of new prospects for the route. Three of them, to be exact. They look good."

I shook my head weakly.

"What a dope," I said. "If I'd had any sense at all, I'd have stayed home and looked after Jamie and made you run the route. We'd probably be rich by now."

"It's not sold yet," Mary-Armour said. "They just *look* like good prospects, that's all. Only we'll have to lower the price a bit."

"Lower away," I said. "From now on I'm going to make my dough lying here in bed."

As might have been expected, two of Mary-Armour's prospects gave her the usual I'll-call-you-later-in-the-week-when-I've-cashed-my-government-bonds routine, and joined the long procession of former prospects who had laughed gaily, waved I.O.U.'s, and finally disappeared into a dense ground fog.

The third prospect, however, hung on. He conducted his negotiations in a pleasant, businesslike manner that was refreshing. He even went so far as to make an offer. Quivering with emotion, the home team made a counteroffer and sat back to wait for his yes or no.

The hot days of summer wore on. I was still in the hospital, and the baby was now more than a month overdue. Our prospect was still mute. Then, on a warm Wednesday in August, I was discharged to continue my recuperation at home.

My hands shook as I packed my bag preparatory to leaving the hospital. My legs shook when I climbed the front steps at home and collapsed into a chair on the porch. I shook all over, but I didn't care. I was home, and I was lucky; the doctors had told me I would have practically no physical impairment from the disease.

The following night, just after dinner, our prospect showed up. We talked for several hours. Finally, at seven and a half minutes after ten, Pacific Daylight Time, our prospect pronounced the historic words: "I'll take it."

The man who left the house at ten-thirty was The New Owner. There were, of course, still contracts to draw up, papers to sign, details to iron out, but we knew The New Owner was a man of honor and would not back out.

At eleven o'clock, as we were getting ready for bed, Mary-Armour said, "Darling, I think we'd better take a ride." Nineteen miles, eight hours, and thirty-eight minutes later, Marie-Louise Nelson weighed in at just over nine pounds.

The autumn was warm and dry and clear, crisp enough in the evening to burn big chunks of eucalyptus wood in the living-room fireplace. The rains came on slowly, giving us plenty of preliminary warning to bring in the tricycle and wagon that had stood out all during the long, rainless summer, to roll up car windows at night, to make sure every member of the family was equipped with boots and a raincoat.

We had a lot of time to think about the gumball business, too, especially while we caught up on our back accounting and paid our last sales tax to the State of California. You couldn't really say much moneywise for the dear old route when you looked at those final figures. It was now all too clear how much capital we'd lost in the venture.

"You know," I said to Mary-Armour, "I remember that Chugwater character telling me that routes built by No-Name were almost never for sale at a figure as low as their original purchase price."

"Good old Og," Mary-Armour said.

I looked up from my sheet of figures to find she was laughing. After a moment, I started to laugh, too.

"Yes," I agreed, "good old Og."

The crazy thing was, we both sort of meant it. Somehow, neither of us could feel very bitter toward the old boy, nor toward cadaverous old Truss, nor treacherous old Gideon, nor anyone. There was too much on the other side of the balance for that. For one thing, there was the experience we'd had; it had been challenging, and a lot of it had been good fun. Besides, we'd learned a very valuable lesson—that we weren't half as smart as we had thought. And then, on top of that, there were the friends we'd made, a whole troop of fine, upright, sincere people.

Take Freddie Wing Duck, for example, the tiny, restless grocer who had given us Cleo; in our scales little Freddie could easily outweigh a dozen overstuffed Og Chugwaters. And fifteen-year-old Ben Thurlow—he canceled out Truslow Thomas, with plenty to spare.

How, in fact, could any gumball magnate dwell on the few disagreeable Gideons when there were so many friendly, decent people to think about, like Joe Lopez y

Garcia, padding about in his open-toed *huaraches*, deploring things; or Jotto Baker, the wild aviator (he finally calmed down about being fired at, incidentally); or M. Montreux, the genial vintner; or poor, ancient, dignified, bankrupt Mr. Watanabe; or old Mrs. Mather, whose anniversary slug of Old Taylor revived my flagging belief in the nobility of mankind; or even friendly, ape-like Dilley Stark, the No-Name employee who unknowingly catapulted us into the carded-goods business; or the shapely, silent Moonstone.

For every painful encounter with an outraged grocer, there were a hundred pleasant conversations to remember. For every rainy day, there were a dozen sunny ones. For every night of despair, Mary-Armour and I could look back on countless pleasant evenings when we had sat side by side at the kitchen table, stuffing Boston Bean globes with charms we *knew* would make our sales double or treble within a matter of days.

And then, too, there was the mobile that hung in our living room to show that the ideal of Time-To-Do-Things had not failed entirely; and the half-dozen home-made, high-fired ash trays scattered around the house, and the remnants of the silk-screen experiment, and the prints, still unframed, from the venture into drypoint etching; and the shelves of books read, and the numberless games of Backgammon and Go that Mary-Armour and I had played, and the hours spent together and with our growing son. No promoter, no competitor, no dismal profit-and-loss statement could ever take these away from us.

October passed, and November, and then came a wet December night that I remember well.

Outside, the black rain was pelting down fiercely. Inside, the fire was blazing away and spitting contemptuously at the rug. Jamie was busy tormenting Cleo, and Mary-Armour was giving the baby her first taste of applesauce. I sprawled in my customary easy chair—I was now Captain

Gumball (Ret.)—and stared into the fire, daydreaming over a half-crumpled newspaper.

"You know, sweetie," I said, as the flames licked at the heaped logs, "I sort of feel like a millionaire, don't you? I mean, now that we've got money in the bank again?"

"It's a nice feeling, all right," Mary-Armour said.

"Of course, we can't live forever on the proceeds from selling the route," I said, "but it feels darn good to know that the wolf can't get at us—at least not for a while anyhow."

A log popped noisily in the fireplace, and a shower of sparks flew up the chimney. Jamie continued to roll on Cleo's stomach, and Mary-Armour troweled applesauce into the baby's mouth with the skill of a master plasterer. I kicked off my shoes and edged my feet closer to the fire. Then I turned toward Mary-Armour.

"How big is our cellar, would you say?" I asked.

Mary-Armour looked up at me briefly.

"It's not really a cellar at all," she said. "It's just an oversized dirt-floor crawl space. Why?"

"Oh, nothing," I said. I loosened my necktie. Mary-Armour went back to her feeding task.

"We're certainly lucky to live in such a fertile spot, aren't we," I said. "You know what Luther Burbank said about this area?"

Mary-Armour stopped feeding the baby and laid down her spoon. She looked me squarely in the eye.

"What are you driving at?" she said.

"Not a thing, really," I said. "I was just thinking, that's all."

"And what were you thinking, if I may ask?"

"Oh, not much," I said, "except that with all this fertile soil under the house . . . Well, what I mean is, listen to this."

I picked up the newspaper and folded it open to the

classified ads. I ran my finger down the page until I found the one I was looking for, and then I read aloud:

" 'Why delay prosperity? Make big money NOW raising giant mushrooms in cellar or basement. Full or spare time. Vast market potential in selling to clubs and restaurants. Small investment provides initial spawn to set you up in this lucrative . . .' "

I heard a snort from across the room and looked up to see Mary-Armour staring at me as though I were a stranger. Then she shut her eyes and began to shake her head back and forth, very slowly.

"Is something the matter?" I said.

Mary-Armour opened her eyes but kept on shaking her head, and then after a while the corners of her pretty mouth turned up in a kind of wistful little smile. She smiled at me this way for a few moments, with her head still shaking, and then she sighed and picked up the spoon and started to feed the baby again.

"No, darling," she said finally, "nothing's the matter. Read me the rest."

ABOUT THE AUTHOR

JIM NELSON, *with his wife and three quite small children, lives now in Northern California, keeping an eye out for any new opportunity in individual enterprise which might present itself. He was born in Denver, educated at New Haven, and employed for some years in New York City as an editor at* Business Week *magazine. His job there, he reports, led him to interview an almost infinite number of tycoons, but as he listened, Nelson's mind apparently wandered, and, as he reports: "As each one, with becoming modesty, described the clever way he had put himself and his cozy little cartel on top of the heap, I often found myself wondering why I was just* writing *about these profitable businesses. Why wasn't I in there restraining trade myself?"*

From such revolutionary thoughts it was but a small jump to gumballs, and life as a minor-league tycoon.

Made in the USA
San Bernardino, CA
23 May 2014